RAINCOAST CHRONICLES

FORGOTTEN VILLAGES OF THE BC COAST

EDITED BY HOWARD WHITE

Harbour Publishing

Forgotten Villages of the BC Coast
Copyright © Harbour Publishing 1987

Editor Howard White   **Editorial Assistant** Audrey McClellan
Associate Editor Peter Trower   **Design** by Gaye Hammond

Published by Harbour Publishing Co. Ltd., Box 219, Madeira Park, BC, Canada, V0N 2H0
Printed and bound in Canada

Reprinted August 1991

All manuscripts should be submitted to the editor at the above address. Unused material will be returned. This publication has been financially assisted by the Government of British Columbia through the British Columbia Heritage Trust.

Photo credits:
Lillian Bateman, 1, 7, 8, 9; Barry Brower, 56; Shirley Corbett, 26 (b), 27; William Hagelund, 66; Harbour Publishing, 25; K. Kadota, 31 (b); Angela Newitt, 16, 17, 18, 20, 21, 22, 23, 24; Harry Osselton, 61; Tom Parkin, 34; Provincial Archives of BC, 5, 6, 11, 12, 14, 15, 26 (t), 28, 29, 32, 51, 53, 59, 60; Jim Spilsbury, 73; Francis Stone, 52, 54; Vancouver Maritime Museum, 63; Vancouver Maritime Museum/Boorman, 64; Jean Wallbank, 30, 31 (t, m); Charlie Watson, 62; Howard White, 39, 35, 43.

CANADIAN CATALOGUING IN PUBLICATION DATA
Main entry under title

Forgotten villages of the BC coast

(Raincoast chronicles, ISSN 0315-2804 ; 11)
ISBN 0-920080-40-5

1. British Columbia—History, Local. 2. Villages—British Columbia—History. 3. Pacific Coast (B.C.)—History. 4. British Columbia—Social life and customs. I. White, Howard, 1945— . II. Series.
FC3817.3.F67 1987   971.1'32   C87-091393-X
F1087.F67 1987

CONTENTS

STORIES OF THE
HORSESHOE VALLEY
THE MOVE NORTH 1920

LILLIAN BATEMAN

WHENEVER CANADIANS ASKED my mother why we had left Seattle, she would reply, quite seriously, that it certainly had not been her idea. It was Father's...him and his doggone bagpipes! Naturally this answer raised more eyebrows and questions, so she explained Dad had been a member of the Seattle Pipe Band when they came up to Vancouver for their annual competition. She added that was the year the Seattle band finally won the silver cup, and Dad had returned in high spirits. For weeks she heard nothing but how wonderful it was up in B.C. It was the land of opportunity. A man could make something of himself there. B.C. had a future. It was the only place to be.

Mother had heard this line before, so she knew what to expect next. Dad was building up to go off on another of his wild goose chases. He was always looking for the "green grass on some far away hill," so she was not surprised when he came from work in the middle of the day to announce he had quit Todd Shipyards. He said he was fed up with Seattle, and it was time for a change. We would pack up and go north this time, back to Canada. Back to God's country. He had decided that Vancouver would be our first stop.

Mother did not want to leave Seattle. She had been happy there the past eighteen months. The fine stores downtown, the mild weather, the flowers, and even the rain were such a relief after

1

living on the Nevada desert. She said she might have refused to move, let Dad go off on his own, but for the fact he would be crossing the line. Dad might not be allowed back in the States. He was a Canadian by birth and had never taken out U.S. papers, in spite of the fact he had lived there twelve years. Mother was also a Canadian so, with this in mind, she agreed we would go along.

There is no official record of our crossing. My year-old brother, myself (age seven, less a month), and my parents came up on the train as tourists, coming to visit friends. Dad shipped all our household effects and a bit of furniture by boat, and I have the old bill of lading, dated August 24, 1920, to prove it. How he managed to get it through Customs is a mystery.

Dad found a place close to Vancouver, where he could leave us while he went off to look the country over. He wasted no time picking and choosing. I'm sure he took the first two-room shack he was offered. It was on Royal Oak Avenue in Burnaby.

When Mother saw the place that Dad expected us to live in, her face fell. There was no bathroom, no tub, no basin, and no toilet. We had to use a wood hut out in the backyard. There was no hot water tank. A single cold tap dripped in a primitive tin sink.

Of course Dad was apologetic; he tried to reassure Mother by saying it was only temporary. "Just hold on till I get settled," he pleaded.

As soon as we were moved in, before we had properly unpacked, Dad took off. He said he would write to let us know where he was. He would report back as soon as he found a job. He seemed positively cheerful as he kissed us good-bye, telling me to be good and Mother not to worry. He might as well have told her not to breathe.

Somehow Mother managed to cope; she got us settled. From this miserable little shack in the brush on an uncleared lot in Burnaby, she sent me off to school for the very first time. I should have been in school in Seattle, but my parents thought I was too small...or I may have been handy as a built-in babysitter. Perhaps it was because I had learned to read and print when I was three. Perhaps it was Dad's idea. He said he didn't want Them filling my head with their Capitalist ideas. Anyway, I fell in love with my teacher and fell in love with school. Anne Forrest was a remarkable teacher, a truly dedicated woman. I still feel privileged to have been one of her pupils. And school was easy. I had the basics already; now I had games to play, songs to sing, and all sorts of new activities. I relished every minute of every day at school, and hated the weekends. Altogether, this was one of the happiest times of my life—and one of the shortest.

Days went by and Dad had not written. Mother did not know where he was and began to worry.

Sammy took a cold, it got worse, and now she really had her hands full. One night he could scarcely breathe, he felt like he was burning up with fever as he choked, cried, and moaned. Mother was up all night, and I was awake most of it. I heard her steady incantation, "Come home, Sam," even in my sleep. She did not know where to turn for help. We had no phone, knew no doctor, knew no neighbour close to us. All she could do was summon Dad home mentally.

It was barely daylight when I got out of bed and came to stand by Mother at the window. She had Sammy in her arms and was watching the path to the street. I asked what she was looking at. She said Daddy should have caught this train out if he came down on last night's boat. It made no sense, but I stared out into the morning mist myself. Then, like a figure in a dream, Dad appeared out of the fog. He came up the path carefully, as though he were trying to come in quietly to surprise us. I sprang to open the door, Mother said, "Thank God you've got here at last," and he stood staring at us as if he had lost his mind.

When things calmed down he had his own story to tell.

He was shaving in the bunkhouse when he heard the boat at the dock below give its early warning toot for the passengers to get aboard. The next thing he knew, he had thrown his razor in the washbasin, grabbed a coat, and was running down the dock. He barely had time to make the gangplank before they hauled it up. As the boat pulled out, he began to collect his wits and couldn't figure out what in blazes he had done this for. None of it made sense. But there he was, on his way to town with only the clothes he stood up in and a few dollars in his pants pocket.

Dad had strange hunches all of his life. He often seemed to read Mother's mind—she could never surprise him—and this may be the reason for his strange behaviour that brought help when we needed it most.

Whatever it was, Dad got a doctor, and Sammy got medication and recovered in no time. Dad's visit alone had more effect on Sammy than anything a doctor could prescribe. He truly missed his father.

Dad's visit was a short one. He had to get back on the job. He was "pattern maker" in the Stillwater machine shop, making the wood forms for castings of gears, shafts, and parts for locomotives and engines. His long training as a cabinet maker had come in handy at last.

Now there was only one more problem to solve. He had to find a place for us to live. There was nothing around Stillwater, but he would keep trying. Mother was patient. She said at least she knew where to reach him now if anything else happened. I was more than willing to stay where we were; I was having a good time at school. I had never had such a variety of kids to play with before. Any place we had lived, Mother had monitored my companions and made her own rules. Her ideas of proper behaviour for little girls were strictly Victorian. Things were not like that at school.

So, when Dad's letter arrived, I felt less than ecstatic. He wrote that he had found a fine place, a homestead—he called it a government pre-emption. He said it was about fifteen miles up the logging train track from the camp at Stillwater, in a place called Horseshoe Valley. We would have no neighbours except an old bachelor on the homestead next to us. There was no house, either. He would have to build one, but that would be easy. There were lots of cedar snags he could cut down to make shakes. Imagine that! A place where you could make your own lumber! And he was still on the lookout for something for us to live in for the winter.

Next mail delivery brought a short note. "Start packing. Found a shack. Be down soon. Dad."

I had never been unduly concerned when Dad uprooted us before, but this time it was different. I resented his interrupting my own life. I wanted to stay where I was and go to school. This move would spoil everything. I wished he had not been able to find a house. I wished we had to stay where we were. I even hoped he would get mad and quit his job. He had done that enough times before, why couldn't it happen now?

When I tried to share these feelings with Mother, she accused me of being selfish; she even suggested I didn't love my daddy. I made an effort to explain it wasn't like that. I still loved Daddy very much; what I hated was leaving Miss Forrest and having to quit school. Mother didn't say much after that outburst. She sighed a lot and went on with the packing.

Dad arrived even sooner than we expected, sooner than I hoped. I went off to school for the last time, said a tearful goodbye to my beloved teacher, and dragged my reluctant feet home to face another move...north.

FROM THEN ON IT was all rush, rush, rush. Everything had to be done in a hurry. Our few sticks of furniture were crated, bedding baled and bundled, dishes boxed, and stove dismantled. Mother went to Vancouver to order our winter supply of groceries. She bought flour, sugar, rice, canned milk, raisins, dried apples...the works. She arranged for Woodwords to ship it up the same day we sailed. Dad insisted on buying three yellow oilskin raincoats he called "slickers." Mother refused hers, said she would not be caught dead in such a thing. Both mine and Sammy's were large and long, stiff, noisy, and smelly. Dad also put my small feet in big boy's boots. They had hobnails on the bottom, a buckled strap on top, and plenty of laces in-between. I would need them in the woods, he said.

The afternoon before our departure, Dad had a van pick up our freight and deliver it to the Union Steamship dock, where it would be loaded on the *Chilco* next morning. We would be travelling up on the same ship, boarding it before nine in the morning. Dad said it was a full day's trip up the coast to Stillwater, because we stopped along the way.

I was apprehensive about this trip, never having been on a boat before—not even in a rowboat or a canoe. Horses and wagons were more my style, something with four feet or four wheels on the solid ground. Perhaps if it hadn't been such miserable November weather I might have been able to enjoy this adventure, but B.C. rain can dampen anyone's spirits. It was still pouring when we locked the door of the little house and set off for the Royal Oak tram station to catch the 4 p.m. Central Park car. Once we arrived downtown we found a cheap hotel near the docks, and went for supper at the White Lunch. If I was silent and gloomy, Mother pale and exhausted, Sammy tired and whining, Dad made enough enthusiastic conversation for all of us.

He was simply brimming with fine plans for the future. He said he had it all mapped out—everything. Once I interrupted him to ask where I would be going to school and it seemed to annoy him. He said I would get all the education I'd need by mail. The government sent correspondence lessons to kids out in the woods. I thought about that for a minute and said it sure didn't sound like much fun.

Mother had her own questions to ask. She wanted details. She had heard about the homestead, that it was right on the logging train track, there was no creek, we would have to carry water from across the track, and there were no near neighbours. Now she wanted to know exactly where he had decided to house us for the winter.

Dad admitted it wasn't much. It had been abandoned when they moved the logging operations. They had taken the bunkhouses but left a cookhouse. He found out about it from someone who heard him say he couldn't find a place for his family. He had gone up to look it over and figured he could fix it up so it would do to "hole up in" for the winter, and give him time to get the house built on the homestead. Handy, too, only about a mile or so down the track from our property...oh, not on the track, of course. It was a quarter mile, he guessed, back in the bush. Neighbours? Well, there were two Irish brothers, Mike and Dinny O'Connel, who lived back closer to the mountain on the other side of the tracks. Mike was a fine fellow, but Dinny was a shy sort. People said he was scared of women. Did he have permission to live in the place? Sure, he had asked the superintendent who said we could use it rent free.

Mother was pretty quiet after that. In all the excitement of packing she had just assumed he had found something near where he worked. He had said it was only a shack, and she'd accepted that fact—he'd put us in some pretty strange places before—but if this cookhouse was where she figured, Dad wouldn't get home every night. We would not see him until weekends. He admitted that would be a problem, but if she could put up with that this winter, he would make it up to her in spring when he would lay off work to build the house.

By the time we had finished eating, everyone was willing to go to bed. It had been a long, hard day for all of us.

I would give a lot to know what thoughts went through my mother's mind that night in the cheap little hotel. None of us slept soundly. The room was warm and stuffy, but opening the window let in too much noise and city smoke and soot. We seemed to sort ourselves out in slow-motion in the morning. Sammy fussed, Dad was impatient, and Mother complained of a headache. Finally we got out on the street and tramped back to the old White Lunch, where Dad insisted they made the only decent coffee in town. I wasn't hungry; I was still tired.

Finishing what passed for breakfast, we returned to the hotel for our baggage, then left for the docks. There was plenty of time before the boat sailed, but Dad had to make sure of the freight.

It was a dark, wet, blustery morning. Sodden papers blew clumsily along the uneven pavement. I followed Dad's yellow reflection, his slicker shining in the large sooty puddles, as I plodded behind in gumboots at least two sizes too large. Once we reached the wharf, Dad parked us in a waiting room while he attended to our tickets and went to look after the freight. He had to be sure it went up with us or "We'd be in a helluva fix," as he put it.

On his return, relaxed and smiling, he suggested we take a look around before we went aboard. Mother elected to stay put, but I was curious and happy to get away from the smoke in the waiting room, so I followed Dad out. I had never actually been on a dock before. In Seattle I had been down to Pike Street Market with Mother, but we never went out on a pier to watch the ships. It was all very strange...the sounds, the winches, the slings of freight being hoisted, boat whistles, bells, men's shouts...but what impressed me most was the smell. When I got a particularly "fruity" whiff I almost choked. Holding my nose I asked Dad, "What's that awful stink?" He laughed and explained it was the mixture of coal smoke, oil, dead fish, kelp, creosote, and garbage, but once we cleared the harbour I would really smell the sea. He said I would like that, and then warned me not to let Mother hear me say stink or she'd "skivver" me.

We passed the *Chilco* and noticed they were getting the gangplank cleared for boarding, so Dad thought we had better collect the others and go aboard. Climbing up a gangplank in loose rubber boots is not the easiest thing in the world; neither is negotiating the high doorsill of a ship. I tripped and came in sprawling, to Mother's annoyance and Dad's delight. He helped me up, laughed, and called me a "landlubber," one who had just been initiated. My knee hurt. I rubbed it, red-faced and embarrassed, hoping no one had witnessed my clumsiness, though I dared not raise my head to find out.

When Dad got us settled comfortably on the old red upholstery, he suggested I come out with him to watch them load the freight. That sounded like a fine idea to me...indoors I would have had to keep an eye on my brother. This time I managed the high sill, and asked why they built them like that. Dad's explanation, about the high seas sweeping along the deck, did nothing to convince me this was going to be a fun trip. We stood at the rail, and I still remember the flood of information Dad poured into my ears. I heard that the hole in the deck was a hatch on top and the hold below. Those were capstans, that was a davit, there was the bow, back behind us the stern, this was port, that was starboard (he pronounced it "stabbard"), and ever so much more of his own adventures aboard a ship in the Atlantic.

We watched them cast off, reverse and "back water," swing the bow northwest, and head for the Narrows. There was no Lion's Gate Bridge hanging in the sky that day; it wouldn't appear for another fifteen years. Behind us the skyline faded away in the rain. The largest and last building that I recall was the Bekin's Building, now the Sun Tower. Dad pointed out Siwash Rock, Prospect Point, the Point Atkinson light...but he was losing his audience. I watched the waves. They were getting bigger and grey, and white-capped rollers swept up the gulf. Dad said we had a sou'easter blowing—we would have a "following sea." I tried to keep my teeth from chattering long enough to say, "Can I go in now, please?" So he took me in, where I stayed until we docked in Stillwater.

It was a long, tiresome day. About three o'clock we reached Sechelt. There was a great deal of freight to unload, and this pier was facing the gulf, so the south-easters blew right in. Our following sea had caught up to us. Moored to the dock, the ship rolled mercilessly. I had been lying down and things began to look funny. I began to feel pretty strange too. Mother must have been keeping an eye on me, because when I reached a suspicious tint of green, she grabbed me and steered for the ladies washroom. There I made my first offering to whichever Sea God was on watch that day. Later I dozed, wished I was dead, wished we had never left home, wished I was anywhere but on this darn boat.

About seven or eight o'clock Dad woke me. He said we would be docking in a few minutes and I had better get my things together. I tried to look out of the window, but the rain blurred everything. All I could make out were a few distant lights and a great deal of blackness I took to be water. Mother buttoned me into my coat, added the slicker, and I followed her out onto the wet deck. I stood shivering, watching the deckhands lower the gangplank. It seemed steep and dangerous in the pitch black night. A couple of floodlights were focused on the unloading; below me, mysterious figures in black raincoats ran about, shouting warnings and orders. Some caught the sling of freight. The scene became unreal, something from another world. I felt I must be dreaming.

Dad and Mother were already on the gangplank. I stood uncertain, confused, watching them descend. Someone behind me nudged me along, steadied me as I took one hesitant step after another. Finally I found myself standing beside Mother. Dad had disappeared into the dark. She told me he had only gone to borrow a lantern. A light moved

towards us and Dad's yellow slicker flickered as he walked, identifying him for us before he spoke. He said we should follow him single-file up the dock, staying close together and keeping to the left. There was a rail on that side, but on the right there was a drop to the ties and the train track. This was where they ran the log cars out before dumping them in the chuck below. I could hear the water sloshing against the piles, which creaked and groaned. Then I thought I heard an engine puffing somewhere up ahead, the pier began to move, and Dad told us to stop and stay close to the hand rail while a train backed down to pick up the freight. A dark shape moved toward us, blotting out the distant lights. A box car slid past, then flat cars. When they screeched to a halt we moved on, passing so close to the huge, hot engine that I might have reached out to touch it. It felt very comforting, like an old friend. I was familiar with trains and liked them very much, so while I walked past the big black shape my fears fell away; I was back on solid ground. Once we were past the engine, its headlight brightened our path. It

Stillwater, 1926

5

Brooks, Scanlon & O'Brian camp at Stillwater, 1926

was easier to follow Dad's yellow slicker, and I could see we would soon be off the pier.

That old yellow slicker moving ahead of me through the blackness of the dock became the focus of this whole unforgettable childhood experience. Later, whenever I saw one on the street, I would be instantly whipped back in time to this, the most disturbing and frightening night of my life. No wonder I never wore mine ever again.

It was at least ten o'clock before the train came back up the dock and began switching for the long haul into the mountains. Dad collected us and our belongings, and herded us out beside the track, where a brakeman stood waving a lantern. When the box car rolled up, he stopped the train and boosted us aboard to Dad, who had hung his lantern on a spike inside the door. We clambered in, someone slammed the big door, Dad said "Sit down before you fall down," the train gave a lurch, and we were on our way. I sat on a box, listened to the familiar noises, felt the familiar motion, and was comfortable for the first time in the entire day. There was nothing to see, just the piled-up freight, so I

must have dozed. It was hard to gather my wits when Dad shook me. He had already opened the door, the train had stopped. Outside I could hear strange voices. Dad handed me down to a tall man in a Mackinaw. He smelled good, like pipe tobacco. Mother stood back in the shadow with Sammy while the men handed down the bales and boxes. All our worldly goods collected in a pile by the track, out in the woods, out in the silently falling rain. I could see no lighted window, no glimmer anywhere between the trees, nothing but the empty darkness. I wondered where we would sleep tonight; peering into the blackness gave me a hollow, lost feeling. Anything could have made me cry. I wondered if we *were* lost.

The two men who had appeared to help with our freight turned out to be our neighbours, Mike and Dinny. Mike was the one who smoked the pipe, the man who lifted me out of the box car. I had a lot of trouble understanding what he said at first—his Irish brogue was something I would learn to admire and enjoy later. He seemed to have taken charge; he was even telling my father what to do. Tarps had appeared and were thrown

6

Cookhouse, November 1920

over the freight. It would be safe in these woods, there was nothing or no one to harm it. Tonight we were going home with Mike. He had it all arranged. Mother, Sammy, and I could have his bunk and Dinny's, he and Dad could sleep on the floor, and Dinny could go to the barn. After warm cocoa and good home-baked bread (Dinny could beat any woman at bread making) we were tucked in. I knew nothing more until the smell of frying hotcakes woke me. I lay quiet, admiring the deer skins, the fine peeled, polished logs, the coat rack of antlers, and listened to Mike as he poured the morning coffee.

As soon as we had had breakfast we left the cabin and followed Dad out to the tracks. Dad said Mike and Dinny would be along later; he wanted to get us and our bags over to the old cookhouse before they started bringing our belongings in. And Mother had better dig out the broom; she would need it.

We followed an old moss-grown, ancient skid-road through the forest. There were many big firs and a few cedars still standing, but most of the best trees had been logged off, and the area was now overgrown with alder. One thing we would never run short of was wood, Dad said. The cookhouse appeared on our right. It too was crowded by the fast-growing alders. Leafless now, they seemed to interlace their branches right over the roof, on which they had laid a matting of wet, dead leaves. It was a discouraging sight. Torn tar-paper on the outside; dirt, dead leaves, evidence of rats inside. Mother and I set about cleaning. By the time the men arrived with an old sledge they had rigged up to haul things, we had the worst swept out. The stove always went up first in a situation like this, and the kettle followed. Dad told me where I would find the creek; water was no problem. It was a hard day's work, but by bedtime we had our own beds to crawl into. Dad said it was smaller than he had thought. We would be pretty crowded, but he had seen an old shed out back. He might just move it up against the cookhouse, cut a hole in the wall, and give me my own bedroom.

As he dimmed the kerosene lamp prior to blowing it out, I looked around the room. It looked cosy and comfortable, even if a bit crowded. There was Mother's little rocking chair, the old table, her sewing machine, Sammy's highchair. I pulled my black-and-white check blanket over my head and fell asleep.

7

LADDIE

DECEMBER 24, 1920. Tomorrow would be Christmas, our first Canadian Christmas. Of necessity, it would be a simple one. Mother had already warned my brother and I that Santa might not find our little shack buried in the B.C. forest. Even if he did spot us, it was more than likely his sack would be empty by that time.

Sammy, not yet two, looked disappointed. He had heard enough of my stories of reindeer and flying sleighs to half believe in a real Santa Claus. At seven I knew better. Santa was only my dad.

Mother looked down at our sober little faces and relented. "Well, you can hang up your stockings at least. There's always a chance that he'll find us." She paused, looked out the window at the swirling snow. "In the meantime you'd better pray that this storm lets up or Daddy might not get home."

I went to the small window to see for myself. The heavy snow had fallen steadily all afternoon. Now all traces of a path had disappeared. It was growing dark and still there was no sign of Father.

Indoors, Mother and I had done our best to welcome him home. We had cut a lovely little fir tree to perfume the air, and had decked it out in all our old familiar treasures. True, the angel looked a bit tired, its tinsel dull and tattered. Our tiny red-felt Santa had definitely seen better days, but the strings of golden balls still glittered bravely as they reflected back the yellow lamplight. Most of them, in spite of our many moves, had survived. Where branches appeared too green and bare, Mother had placed bright old-fashioned cards, keepsakes from the Boston years. I had painstakingly cut and glued a red paper garland to drape around the lowest boughs. Then came the candles. As I carefully fastened their metal clips to the ends of branches, I wished we could light them, just once...even one single, solitary candle. I asked Mother. I should have known better. It only started her on her stories about trees alight, houses burning, and children being destroyed.

Finally we were finished and stood back to admire the tree and discuss the stockings. We decided to wait until bedtime before hanging them up behind the heater. That was as close to a chimney as we would ever get in this place. Perhaps, I told my little brother, if Santa did come, we would find a nice red apple or an orange, maybe a handful of nuts and a striped candy cane in the morning. We might even get a real surprise. But of course, Daddy had to make it home first. There could be no Christmas without him.

All day our conversation had centered around Father. When would he arrive? What might he bring? Would he like our tree?

The Lamont family

Now, with the snow sill falling, we began to have doubts. Could he walk the six miles up from camp in this weather? Mother said she doubted it, not in such a storm, not in the dark. There were the trestles. I thought of the snow covering the slippery ties, and of the white water of the Eagle River far below. I began to hope he would play it safe and wait until morning.

Weekdays he worked in the big machine shop at the edge of the wharf in Stillwater. When he came home to visit, he tried to catch a ride up on the speeder or a late train, but tonight there would be no train. Everyone would have gone home early to be with family, or was off to Vancouver for a logger's spree. If he planned to get home tonight, he would have to walk, and it was a stiff grade every step of the way to the trestles.

Mother told us if Daddy left camp at five he would likely be home before ten at the latest. We ate a silent supper, our ears tuned to the world of snow outside, hoping to hear a footfall, a bang on the door. Sammy grew sleepy and was tucked into bed. Mother and I sat close to the heater, quiet, listening to the whine of wind and hiss of snow against the window. Ten o'clock came and went. I began to droop. Mother told me to go to bed. She put another stick of wood into the fire and resumed her silent vigil, wrapped in her private thoughts. She hardly heard me say goodnight as I kissed her cheek.

Suddenly, about midnight, there was a lull in the storm. The silence wakened me. I was lying listening to the quiet when I thought I heard a scuffling, shuffling noise, and a couple of solid thumps.

"Dad!" I screamed, and leapt out of bed, wide awake, my heart pounding. I was just in time to see a grotesque, snow-covered figure stagger into the room. A blast of cold air and a swirl of snow followed. He stood hunched over, puffing, quite out of breath, and stamped his feet about as if to make sure he was on a solid floor. So far he had said nothing, nor had we. We were awed by this figure and waited for it to speak. Abruptly he bent over, opened his Mackinaw, and a shapeless brindle bundle dropped to the floor. Now we were truly speechless. The object reassembled itself into a puppy right before our eyes. What a dog. A blonde, brindled, flop-eared, black-muzzled creature with a rubber band for a spine. He wriggled, twisted, and contorted until his whole hide seemed to undulate. The rolling wrinkles came to an abrupt end at the stub of a tail he was trying so hard to wag in greeting.

By now Sammy had joined us. He rubbed his sleepy eyes; they grew rounder and bluer than ever. His mouth fell open. "A DOG!" he barely whispered, then, "Gee! What's his name?"

While Dad removed his wet Mackinaw and started to work at the boots, we all flung questions. "Where did you get him? How'd you ever get him home? How old is he? Did he have to walk in all that snow?"

Looking serious, practical Mother said, "Is he housebroken?"

Dad said the pup was about four months old; his name was Laddie; he was part bulldog, part Airedale; he was housebroken; he walked most of the way, but had to be carried over the trestles, where Dad almost lost him between the ties. Dad buttoned him inside his jacket most of the rest of the way home. The dog was getting played out and slowing him down.

Mother wanted to know how Dad got him, so he had to confess Laddie was given away by a fellow in camp who was going to "knock him in the head." Sammy and I gasped at this news, but Mother sensibly asked, "Why?"

By this time my brother and I were on the floor with the dog, sharing his wet kisses. Dad was still struggling out of his high boots. "Oh," he said, between puffs, "this guy has a kid, little girl about as old as Sammy here, and the damn dog kept knocking her down. The kid would barely get on her feet when Laddie here would run and jump on her. . .figured it was some sort of game. Anyway, this guy's wife said the dog had to go, she'd had enough of howling kids. Nobody at camp would take him, not with that habit. So, here he is. Guess I didn't like the idea of him killing the dog. That's it." He stood up, looked at Mother's doubtful face and then at Sammy, rolling about with the dog.

"We'll soon take care of that jumping-up business," he announced.

Now Sammy and the dog had begun to play. Laddie dashed off and sat on his haunches about eight feet away. He looked alert and expectant.

Sammy had risen and was about to give chase when the dog launched himself at the boy's chest. Down he went and the dog raced by, turned, and sat poised for a repeat performance as soon as the child got on his feet. Right now Sammy sat red-faced and angry, his eyes watered but he didn't look like he was going to cry. He looked mad. He was slowly beginning to get on his feet when Dad intervened.

"Wait," he cautioned. "Now, take this." He placed the wire-handled, short, steel poker in the boy's hands. "Pay attention, now. Listen. Hold it like this, see? The next time Laddie runs at you, be ready, give him a good whack on the nose, see? Like this." He held the boy's hands around the poker and demonstrated. "That's all. Whammo."

Sammy caught on fast. Armed, he got up slowly, eying the dog all the time. His bright eyes had the glint of battle. Feet apart, he waited for Laddie to make his move.

Accepting the challenge, the dog ran, jumped. . .and suddenly the game took a new twist. The victim had stepped back and swung the poker across the dog's thick skull. For once he was the one to sit down suddenly. He stayed down, shaking his head and looking puzzled, watching the boy with the poker. Whatever he thought, no one knows, but he got the message. He had taken his last jump. You might think he would forget this lesson and return to his old tricks after a few days, but he never did. He was an intelligent dog. One whack from a small boy had solved everything.

He grew into a fine watchdog and playmate. It may have been a poor Christmas in some ways, but I remember it as the best ever. Laddie was the most exciting gift two lonely children ever received.

Laddie

The Fabulous West Coast

AL BLOOM

TO BRITISH COLUMBIANS living in the Vancouver area there was the Fraser River, Burrard Inlet, and Horseshoe Bay. A little further north was the Sechelt Peninsula and the Sunshine Coast. Beyond that was the North Coast. The name West Coast was reserved for the fantastic stretch of rock, water, and trees from Port Renfrew to Cape Scott, the west coast of Vancouver Island. The island is listed as 286 miles long, but the coastline is ten times that length when one goes in and out of the many inlets along the way. The distance from Victoria to Barkley Sound is about 100 miles, and there is not one good harbour for a ship of any size to weather out a storm in the area. Since the days of the sailing ships there have been over 100 vessels wrecked on this treacherous coast: the "Graveyard of the Pacific."

The good ship *Princess Maquinna*, a CPR combination passenger and freight boat, was built in Victoria in 1912 expressly for this West Coast run. She was 232.6 feet long, with a beam of 28 feet, a gross tonnage of 1777 tons, and a speed of 12 to 13 knots. The superstructure was kept to a minimum; there were no promenade decks with large windows, as other CPR ships had. The hatches were forward, and the cabins, smoking lounge, social hall, and dining room were aft of the hatches, the most comfortable part of the ship in a storm. She could handle 400 day passengers but only had about fifty staterooms with upper and lower bunks. There were often many passengers who had to spend the night in one of the lounges, and from 1938 on to 1950 it was impossible to get a room unless you booked weeks in advance, even though the *Princess Norah* was put on the run in the summer to handle the tourist trade.

The *Maquinna* made her maiden voyage on July 20, 1913, and for the next thirty-nine years, except for a few Alaska trips, she went up and down the west coast, from Victoria to Port Alice at the north end of the island, making the trip twice a month. Captain Edward Gillam was her master for the first twenty years, and there were many stormy, foggy days and nights that he guided her in and out of narrow, crooked inlets and around rocky points out into the wild Pacific ocean before

ducking back into a sheltered inlet. He did this in the days when all he had was a whistle, compass, and wireless telegraph; no radio phone, no radar, no depth sounder—all necessary navigational aids today. The *Maquinna* only had a couple of minor accidents, and seldom missed a scheduled stop, regardless of weather.

She was the supply ship for a number of remote settlements. In 1937 there were no roads north or west of Port Alberni except for some logging roads, and no roads of any kind to the West Coast, so the *Maquinna* called at all the villages, and often tied up at docks half the length of the ship, sometimes even to floats at the logging camps. If special arrangements were made in advance, she would stop any place to deliver freight or passengers to a new camp or a boat. At each regular stop the gangway was put ashore first, and there was always a group of people who rushed on board, laughing and talking excitedly, happy for this chance to communicate with the outside world. When the whistle blew for departure, they would stream off again with their books, papers and magazines, and candy. This touch of civilization would hold them for another two weeks, when the boat and its crew would make its next call going north. The boat always called at the same ports on the way south, but by then most of the goodies would be gone, so few people came on board except to mail a letter or do other business, or to make the trip out. Time went fast on the coast because it was governed by the boat, and life was eaten up in ten day gulps.

I FIRST SAW THE *Princess Maquinna* in August 1937 at Port Alberni. I had come from Saskatchewan to get away from the depression, the dust, and the lack of jobs, but I soon found out that Port Alberni was no better, especially for a prairie chicken. At that time there were two major sawmills operating, and they were the only people hiring men in any numbers. To get a job you had to go to the sawmill gate before each change of shift, complete with lunch bucket and work clothes, and join the gang of out-of-work men who made this pilgrimage three times a day, hoping that they were going to take on another man or two for a new project, or that a regular

Princess Maquinna *at Bamfield*

man was sick and unable to come to work. All this for 35 or 40 cents an hour, no unemployment insurance, no pensions, no medical, and when they did get a job, the hard work required around sawmills in those days just about killed them in their weakened condition. The ones that weren't picked, and often that meant everyone, would return to town and try to scrounge a dollar or two doing odd jobs wherever they could find them. It didn't look like my kind of life.

The papers were full of stories of the rich gold mines at Zeballos, and, being a carpenter of sorts, I figured that I would have a better chance of finding work in a boom town. I bought a ticket for a stateroom on the *Maquinna*, en route to Zeballos.

When I boarded the boat that night in late August, I didn't really know what I was heading into. I hadn't seen anything larger than a rowboat since I was six years old. I stood on the deck at midnight as the ship left the dock, watching the Port Alberni lights disappear in the gloom. August was the best month on the coast, and so far I had enjoyed good weather. I had heard that it rained a lot on the West Coast. The figure three hundred inches of rain a year had been mentioned, but I had no conception of what that meant, and I gave no thought to the winter. I was certain that it would be better than the thirty below and lower that I was used to in Saskatchewan.

The water was smooth in Alberni Inlet, and the ship made a pleasant swishing sound as it moved along through the dark. I could see the shape of the tall, steep mountains on both sides of the inlet, starting at the water's edge and reaching to the sky. I climbed into my bunk and slept the sleep of the innocent, to be awakened the next morning by a steward walking up and down the aisles between the cabins, beating out a tune on his chimes and intoning, "First call to breakfast, first call to breakfast. . . ."

I was hungry and answered that call with alacrity. Meals were served in a beautiful, dark-panelled dining room, with several heavy, mahogany tables covered with white linen and set with fine silverware. A ship's officer was at the head of each table. An immaculate waiter took my order and I had a fine breakfast.

The *Maquinna* had three or four stops in Barkley Sound. The main one was Kildonan, the B.C. Packers fish plant, biggest fish processing plant on the West Coast. They canned salmon here, and brought the fish from the entire coast by big packer boats. They also processed pilchards and herring into fish meal and fish oil, and they had a large cold-storage plant to make ice for the boats and for fish storage. B.C. Packers had another reduction plant not far away at Ecoole, and Nelson Brothers had a reduction plant at Toquart. This was my first sight of fish plants and I wasn't much impressed. But if the shore plants,

11

with their white-washed, board and batten walls and rusty, galvanized iron roofs, weren't much to look at, the fish boats were another story. They were kept in good shape, well painted and clean, and looked ready to take on the West Coast storms.

Like all coast canneries, it was a self-contained community, with a store, cookhouse, bunkhouses for both men and women, and a recreation hall. There was also the ever-present Indian village, and the China house. Without the Indian women and the Chinese men, the coast canneries would not have been able to operate.

We left Kildonan on the way to Ucluelet, and could see Bamfield on the south shore, near the entrance to Barkley Sound. This small community played an important role in world affairs for many years after 1900, as it was the terminus and relay station for the trans-Pacific underwater telegraph cable. In 1937 the station employed 45 people, including 24 operators relaying messages around the British Empire. New technology in radio, microwaves, and satellites made this station obsolete in 1959, but the sleepy little fishing village was again rejuvenated in 1971, when five western Canadian universities established a Marine Biological Station at the site of the old telegraph station.

At the north entrance to Barkley Sound we came to a small bay, protected on the southwest by a narrow strip of high ground a couple of miles long, like a miniature Baja peninsula. This was an excellent harbour, about half a mile wide and deep enough for coast freighters. On the eastern shore going north was an Indian settlement, some private property, and the Nootka Packing Company's Port Albion reduction plant. On the west side of the bay we stopped at Ucluelet, with the government dock and the remaining shore taken up with tie-up floats for fish boats. The outer ends of the floats were occupied by fish buying stations and a couple of oil barges. This was the permanent home of many trollers, the majority of them Japanese. They were an industrious group of people, who kept their boats and their homesites in first class condition. They worked hard and made a good living, even though the best price for fish was thirty or forty cents a pound.

On leaving the sheltered bay at Ucluelet, the *Maquinna* made a sharp turn to the right and sailed between jagged rocks that looked very dangerous to a landlubber. Waves were breaking on these rocks and sending spray high into the air. The ship began to roll slightly. As we cleared the rocks and turned in a northerly direction again, we were out on the open ocean, and the long Pacific swells caught the ship broadside. She rolled along in great style. To the west, except for a few trollers that kept disappearing in the trough, only to reappear again on top of the giant waves, there was water as far as the eye could see. To the east was the now-famous Long Beach, although it was many years before the road from Alberni would be built and tourists would flock to Pacific Rim Park. In my time, Long Beach was used as a road between Ucluelet and Tofino, and it made a fine speedway, well maintained by the waves. There were few cars around, and the truck drivers who used the route had to watch for tides. A breakdown with tides coming in spelled doom for the truck; it would be sucked down and covered with sand in short order. Although I worked at both Ucluelet and Tofino, I never did visit the beach. The local people considered it to be a wet, cold, foggy stretch of hard sand that would never amount to much.

Our rolling ride only lasted a couple of hours and was quite pleasant, but during storms this was

Kildonan Cannery

a rough stretch to travel. The waves hit slightly on the stern side and gave the boat an unpleasant twisting, rolling motion. We ducked behind an island and tied up at the Tofino government dock. Tofino was another fishing village, the permanent home of a hundred or so fishermen, both trollers and seiners. It had a good shipyard that was well known on the coast. Residents of Tofino were not as isolated as people north of them, who depended on the *Maquinna* for all contact with the outside. They lived near stores and fish-buying stations, and had access to the M.V. *Uchuck*, a small motor vessel that made regular trips from Ucluelet to Port Alberni with mail, passengers, and freight.

Across the bay from Tofino, about half a mile away, was a fairly large island and a little village called Clayoquot. The island has sandy beaches, and sand bars that reach out into the harbour and make navigation difficult. The *Maquinna* man-euvered to the Clayoquot dock and tied up for a short while. This was an important stop; there was a hotel with a beer parlour here, the only one at that time between Port Alberni and Port Alice. The passengers rushed ashore and returned with cases of beer to provide lubrication for the rest of the trip, and the *Maquinna* waited for them.

After leaving Tofino Harbour the ship worked its way through mostly sheltered waters to Ahousat, on Flores Island, the early home of the famous Gibson brothers—coast loggers, fisher-men, and, later, politicians. This is where the Gibsons lived as teenagers, working in their father's sawmill, cutting and trimming natural crooks from tree roots for the Victoria shipyards. In the early days, the *Maquinna* tied up overnight at Ahousat, and the Gibson boys would escort passengers across the island on plank walks they had built over the wet ground, stopping at the local hot springs for a refreshing dip, then returning to their home, where they danced in the living room to the wee hours of the morning.

The inlet leading to Ahousat was so narrow that the ship had to travel in reverse for half a mile or so on the way out, before there was enough room to turn around. I made the trip one night when it was so dark and foggy that I couldn't see either shore, but the *Maquinna* managed to be right on course and found that little dock, just by giving periodic blasts on the whistle and listening to the echoes. And then she retraced the route in reverse! The crews were fantastic seamen. Someone asked one of the captains how he could remember where all the rocks were and he replied, "I can't. I just know where they aren't."

After leaving Ahousat we were in the open again, heading for Estevan Point, but first we had to drop anchor in Hesquiat Harbour and wait for boats, mostly Indian dugout canoes, to come from shore. As they approached, the freight doors near the water line on the leeside were opened, and freight was passed out by hand to the waiting boats. If there were passengers they had to go the same way, and as there was always a strong swell running, it was a dangerous feat to perform. Hesquiat was an Indian village, but there were also people at the lighthouse on Estevan Point. They all had to get supplies and personnel this hazardous way. During the winter storms the *Maquinna* would often miss this stop and keep well outside of Estevan Point en route to Nootka, a place sheltered by the great bulk of Nootka Island, and made famous by the early explorers who called there to trade with the Indians.

The Nootka Packing Company had a salmon cannery, net loft, reduction plant, and boat repair shops here, with the reduction plant at Port Albion, and their head office in Vancouver. It was a well maintained plant and an efficient opera-tion. Their fleet was small but it was of the highest quality, and the officials were real people. Many years later they sold out to the Canadian Fishing Company, and when Nelson Brothers were bought by B.C. Packers, it left the coast with only two major fishing companies: B.C. Packers and Canadian Fishing Company.

We sailed past a number of tree-covered islands in Nootka Sound, and then turned northwest into Tahsis Inlet, another deep, narrow, winding waterway with tall mountains coming right down to the water. The slopes were covered with trees—fir, hemlock, cedar—and a lot of scrub bush, right down to the high water mark. I soon saw my first small, gyppo logging show (it was anything but small to me) where everything was on big log floats, jill-poked from shore by long logs, and anchored in place with cables running ashore and tied to big stumps. The cookhouse and bunkhouse were on floats, and on another float there was an A frame, made of two heavy poles about one hundred feet high, lashed together at the top and held upright by several cables. At the bottom of the A frame was the donkey engine, powered at first by a steam boiler, but later by the more efficient diesel engine, and connected to a three-drum winch. One drum held the strawline, the second the heavier haulback line, and the third the heavy mainline. When setting up a new show, the light strawline was hauled up the side of the mountain by hand, to the top of the area to be worked. Once the strawline was in place, then the rest of the heavy rigging was hauled up and positioned. The mainline and haulback ran through blocks high up in the A frame, the haulback went through the block at the top of the show and then fastened to the mainline. The mainline dragged the logs down hill to the water and the haulback pulled it, with the chokers flying, back up the mountain for another load.

The A frame shows were tough to work on; you had to be a mountain climber in heavy caulk boots, able to scramble over and under logs, pulling and pushing heavy chokers into position,

Making up a Davis raft

and getting out of the way before the whistle punk started a load on its way down hill. The loggers were a colourful bunch; they worked hard and played hard, and seldom stayed in camp for more than a month or two at one time before heading for town. They would return to Vancouver, lead the life of Riley for a couple of weeks, spend all their money, and then return to camp for another session.

As the *Maquinna* moved through the quiet waters, we passed a couple of these floating rigs, and could see many places where they had been working, taking the easy-to-get logs along the shore. The sides of the mountains were stripped clean of all greenery as far as the mainline cable could reach — usually a few thousand feet — but the hills and valleys away from the water were left for a different breed of logger to come later with his mechanical equipment on caterpillar tracks.

At this time Gibson Brothers had a number of West Coast logging shows, with their main camp at Sandspit in Tahsis Inlet. This camp was all on big floats, one of the *Maquinna*'s regular stops. There was Gordon Gibson standing on the float, a big cigar clamped in the corner of his mouth, but it didn't stop him from roaring a greeting to the captain on the bridge. He was big, burly, loud, the typical bull-of-the-woods if there ever was one, in his bone-dry clothes with the pants stagged halfway up his legs, and his jacket wide open showing the bright, wide braces that he used to hold his pants up. His feet were shoved into high-top caulk boots with the tops wide open and

the laces flying in the breeze, so he could kick them off in a hurry whenever he entered a camp building. His younger brother Earson was beside him, a much better-looking, less abrasive image of Gordon. Then there was Jack, the sophisticated, well-mannered, well-educated smoothy, who later went into federal politics and gave the Gibsons contacts at all levels. When the *Maquinna* docked he would go on board, carrying his caulk boots in his hand, and head downstairs to the lounge, where he put his stocking feet up on a coffee table in a most relaxed manner and enjoyed an hour's conversation with the people around him. The oldest brother, Clarke, took care of the Vancouver office. They couldn't lose, with Gordon to ramrod and bulldoze his way through any job around the woods or on the boats, and the others to smooth over the rough edges he left along the way. Of course, I didn't see all this on my first trip up the coast, but I did find the camp interesting, though it looked a little haywire.

Our next stop was Ceepeecee, where Nelson Brothers had their fish processing plant. Ritchie and Norman Nelson owned and operated this plant — where they canned salmon and processed pilchards and herring into fish meal and fish oil — along with their plant at Prince Rupert and a cannery on the Fraser River. The Nelsons started with a small gillnet boat on the Fraser and became two of the most respected and liked men in the fishing industry, with the third largest fish company on the coast. They seldom came to Ceepeecee, as it was a two-week round trip on the *Maquinna*, but let their manager run the plant. He was Dal Lutes, a character in his own right with a voice and vocabulary that would do justice to a mule skinner, a job that he handled in his younger years when he freighted from Steveston to Vancouver over a wagon road now known as Granville Street. He ran Ceepeecee as if he owned it, and when the only contact with head office was a shortwave radio, it is small wonder that this should be so. To all and sundry, Lutes was Mr. Ceepeecee, loved and respected by many, hated by others. When the *Maquinna* docked, the tourists would flock ashore to stretch their legs. To reach the local store they had to follow a ten-foot-wide plank walkway between the cannery and the reduction plant, plowing their way through various strong smells produced by the reduction plant and by rotting offal on the beach. They covered their noses with perfumed handkerchiefs and rushed through this section, hoping to reach fresh air again.

As we left Ceepeecee we swung left, and soon we could see another settlement around a point of land. This was McBride Bay, on the east coast of Nootka Island, where a big sawmill was under construction. It was to be a modern mill, financed by English money, but at that time it wasn't too impressive. I could see a small sawmill busy cutting lumber for the construction job, and off to the left I saw the heavy timber frame of the new mill. There were some shacks for the construction crew to live in and that was about it. The *Maquinna* had a lot of freight to discharge, so I went ashore to have a look around, and in the process I inquired about a job. Much to my surprise, they were expecting a carpenter on the boat and he hadn't arrived, so they hired me. I went back on board, arranged to have my baggage put ashore, gathered up the stuff that I had in the stateroom, and said goodbye to the ship. I couldn't believe my luck; at a time when thousands of men were out of work, I had just blindly fallen into a good job—one that lasted for ten months. I had found a niche that I liked, and I stayed in that area, working around the camps and the canneries for ten years, and I never once looked for a job; the jobs always found me.

The *Maquinna* finished unloading at McBride Bay and continued on her way to Zeballos, Kyuquot, and Port Alice, with a few intermediate stops as well. Then she started on the return journey, touching all the main stops, meeting all the same people, but, most important, carrying all the letters from coast people to their friends and families in the outside world.

I MADE MY LAST trip on the *Maquinna* in October 1946, when I packed up my family and headed for a dryer climate. The strangest thing was that I didn't really mind the rain that much. It was seldom cold, and everyone just put on rain clothes in the morning and went to work. One November it rained steady and hard, night and day, for thirty days, and dumped about sixty inches of water on us. That was a little much, but when the sun broke through for a few days, everything was forgotten. All we could think of was how wonderful the West Coast really was.

When I left in '46, the *Maquinna* was still the Queen, an institution, a way of life for all West Coasters, but shortly after that the airplanes started to take over. People could get in a plane at any camp and fly direct to Vancouver in an hour or so, whereas it had taken us two days. The glamour was all gone. The loggers, miners, fishermen, and cannery workers, along with the tourists and businessmen, had all dressed up in their finest clothes for two days of elegance and fine meals—a touch of class that the *Maquinna* gave to a group of people whose lives were far from glamorous most of the year.

The *Maquinna* didn't desert the people, the new breed deserted her. First the airplanes. Then the fish on the West Coast became scarce and the canneries shut down; the companies moved their plants to the Fraser River. The mining boom at Zeballos burst and it turned into a ghost town, to be revived later by the loggers. The sawmill at McBride Bay operated for less than a year before

Esperanza Hotel, 1939

it folded; the plant was dismantled, everything was sold, and the site was once more taken over by Mother Nature as she tried to hide the destruction that man had created.

A fine hotel had been built at Esperanza, a few miles across the bay from the sawmill, to tap the mill trade. For several years it was the meeting place for loggers, cannery workers, fishermen, and travelers. It closed its doors before 1950 rolled around, was sold to Dr. McLean, and later burned down. Even Dr. McLean's hospital and church on Esperanza Point, a West Coast institution for many years, fell on hard times and closed its doors. The area from Nootka to Kyuquot has been left entirely in the hands of the loggers, and they have scarred the mountain sides and valleys with their destructive methods of operation. Gibson Brothers built a sawmill at the head of Tahsis Inlet, not more than a dozen miles from the ill-fated McBride Bay sawmill, and it was a fantastic success. There was, and probably still is, a small freight boat travelling from Port Alberni to Zeballos to service the sawmill and loggers, but it is a poor substitute for the *Maquinna* in her glamour days.

An era has gone forever!

The *Maquinna* was scrapped, her superstructure torn off and the interior gutted out, and she became a dirty ore barge that could be seen going up and down the coast on a tow line, her tired hull straining to keep the weight of the ore from springing her poor old seams and sending her to the bottom. Thankfully they changed her name. She became the ore carrier *Taku*, and fell to the shipbreaker's hammer in 1962.

Some Childhood Memories
of CLO'OOSE

ANGELA NEWITT

IN 1914, TRAVELERS ALONG THE life saving trail on Vancouver Island's remote west coast were sometimes astonished to be met by two little girls in white fur coats and hats. Those children were myself and my sister Marguerite. We lived there in a little community called Clo'oose, a community that came into being because of a real estate hoax and today can no longer be found at all.

My parents came to Canada from England in 1911, and on the trip over they made friends with a Welsh family. Two years later, settled in

Medicine Hat, Alberta, they received an impassioned letter from their Welsh friends, asking my mother and father to join them in forming a new community in fabulous virgin country on the seacoast in British Columbia, a community being organized by the impressively-named West Coast Development Company. They were going to Clo'oose, about eighty miles north of Victoria. We were sent masses of literature from the company describing the hotel, the golf course, and the large family houses on the seashore. My parents decided to go, and go we did, stopping

16

Marguerite's christening at Tent Village

only in Victoria on the way to purchase ten acres of land on the Cheewhat River at Clo'oose and two lots to build on behind the beach—all sight unseen, of course.

In those days the only way to get to Clo'oose from Victoria was on the *Tees* or the *Maquinna*, both old tubs that rolled continually in the giant West Coast swells. These boats were met out at sea by an assortment of small dinghys and Indian canoes that rose and fell with the waves as nervous passengers tried to board them. I was only three when we arrived and my baby sister Marguerite was six weeks old, so neither of us remember that first landing, but Mother never forgot how terrified she had been. We were met by a launch, the *Enilada*, and taken into Nitinat Lake, a little late for high tide and just barely avoiding disaster on the hazardous Nitinat Bar. Our Welsh friends were staying in a settler's cabin on the lake, and we were taken in with them for a time.

My parents' dream of waterfront living was the first to be dashed; they found that there was the small matter of a tiny piece of Indian Reserve between our lots and the beach. There were no long wharves with arriving cargo ships and no wide streets running between fine buildings as described in the Development Company's brochures. The promised CNR spur line from Lake Cowichan on the east side of the Island had not been built—and never would be. They were not at all prepared for the total lack of amenities, and for the rough Indian trails which were the only means of communication. Like many of the newcomers, my parents had been taken in by the Company's scheme to develop a summer resort in this forbidding area.

But other settlers were arriving, and it was decided to set up a tent city at the far end of Clo'oose beach until homes could be built. At Tent Village the first item on the agenda was to get my sister christened, and it just happened that a visiting minister, Reverend Littler, arrived in time to perform the ceremony. A table covered with an exquisite lace tablecloth was set up on the sand outside our tent, and pictures were taken with baby in a gorgeous long christening robe that had been mine back in civilized England.

Furniture barge landing on Clo'oose beach

Author's cabin

Everyone pitched in, and before long a respectable number of log cabins replaced the tents. Daddy insisted our cabin must have leaded-glass windows, and created quite a stir by having them shipped up from Victoria. Our furniture arrived on a barge which was beached almost in front of the house. It would have been impossible to transfer such bulky and fragile cargo out at sea, and it was equally impossible to build a pier at Clo'oose, due to the strong Pacific swells that shifted the sand and carried large drift logs to shore. Everybody helped to carry all the pieces up to the cabins. We had a very old grandfather's clock and a large dining room suite, and our Welsh friends, the Meredith-Joneses, had a piano and a Royal Worcester tea set, which was for quite some time displayed on shelves suspended from their tent frame. Mrs. Jones also had damask table cloths and napkins that were in daily use, even though all the washing water had to be hauled from the well and the ironing must have been an awful chore. Years later Mrs. Jones told her daughter that she felt it was important to keep up their morale because if that had gone, so would their courage.

Life settled down, the residents coping as best

18

they could. The only jobs available were for linesmen and government surveyors; later there were some in fishing and the cannery. Daddy joined the rest in whatever jobs the government offered, although he hated work on the telegraph line. Poor Daddy, I don't know what he thought he was going to do in Canada. He had left a nice cushy job with Prudential Life in London, where his hobby was the Royal Horticultural Society and growing prize roses for show. His passport to Canada described him as a "Gentleman Farmer"!

We were entirely dependent on ships calling from Victoria, weather permitting. This was almost never in the winter months, from fall to early April, so we had to order staples and canned and dried goods in large quantities—hundred-pound sacks of sugar and flour and lots of canned milk. My sister was weaned on Eagle Brand condensed milk. We also had large quantities of something called hardtack, and even the dog got some of that. Once when a visitor came to call and asked me what we had for breakfast, I replied, "Well, I have porridge, Mummy has toast, and Daddy has dog biscuits."

We were fairly well supplied in other ways, though, for the unmarried surveyors brought us ducks or bear and deer meat—in return for a homecooked meal. Fish was so plentiful that you couldn't give it away. We had garden vegetables in season, and dandelion greens and young stinging nettles were very healthy additions to our menu. The summer brought raspberries and huckleberries, and there was the ever-popular salal in August for pies, puddings, and wine. I remember my friend Gwynneth and I used to get tummyaches every year by eating salal that was not really ripe. We were shown how to pinch the stem end of the berry to make the petal-like end open up, so we could be sure that there were no worms or insects in it. Once Mother made a batch of salal wine, put it under the house to ferment, and promptly forgot all about it. One day an oldtimer came to call and Mother needed something to offer him. She remembered the brew down below and came back up with a glassful, but our guest claimed that the first sip practically blew his head off!

Our worst problem was the Indian dogs, unfed and running in packs. They were scrawny, light-coloured creatures with pale eyes. My parents brought two goats up from Victoria for fresh milk, along with some bantam chicks for eggs. The chickens were fenced in, but the goats were allowed to wander during the day. I remember so well the morning we couldn't find them. We went to the sand dunes behind the beach and scrambled over the logs. There we found them both, dead and severely mauled by the dogs.

There were also wild predators. Our cabin had a crawl space beneath it where our dog Peter slept. One night there was a terrific commotion below.

Wakened by the snarling, I came padding into the living room in time to see Daddy grab his gun and hear Mother say, "No, Sam, you are *not* going out there." Daddy opened the window and shot an enormous cougar as it crossed the clearing to go back into the woods. But it was too late for poor Peter.

GRADUALLY MORE AND MORE people came until we had a nucleus of forty or fifty. The settlers had to find ways to make their own fun. Sometimes there were gigantic beach bonfires. The men would go down during the day and pile huge logs in preparation. Our parents took us there with them, and as the fire began to die down we were wrapped in blankets and put to sleep on the sand, to be awakened about midnight and carried home. I remember lying there on the beach watching the stars, the first time that I had really been aware of them.

We also had house parties, either at somebody's cabin or at Mrs. Wood's General Store. Once we held a fancy-dress party ourselves and, as always, all of Clo'oose was invited. Mother put up a notice in the store saying Come One, Come All, and on the appointed night everybody came, all in homemade costumes and fully masked. Gwynneth and I were dressed as fairies, in white frocks with sparkling crowns and silver wands. The guests were not to unmask till midnight, and Gwynneth and I had very special permission to stay up only until ten, so we went around climbing up on everyone's knee to peek under their masks until we knew who each one was. All except one. There was a man there in full Indian regalia. He did not speak, but joined in all the games such as darts and bow-and-arrow, and he excelled in all. At midnight he revealed himself to be a genuine Haida Indian, visiting from the Queen Charlotte Islands. He then bowed to everyone and quietly left, one more guest who had seen the invitation in the store. Our little community buzzed for a week about how gentlemanly and good-looking he was.

One of our favourite occupations was to go down to the Cheewhat River and watch the Indians spearing fish as they passed under the little bridge, salmon thick as a carpet. I remember once going for a walk to the Logan's post office, which took us past the Indian village. As we passed the village there was an old Indian woman propped up against the wall of one of the houses, looking very ill. I was most concerned, but my father explained to me that the tribe always put their dying outside their homes, for fear that evil spirits might enter as she left. I still thought it was very sad.

We also made a trip to the Nitinat Cannery at Brown's Bay, a two-mile walk over slippery logs and many mud puddles. My main memory of that was the awful smell of the place.

I have a picture of another day, when my sister

Mr. Brown of Brown's Bay

and I got all dressed up to go and have tea with Mr. Brown, after whom Brown's Bay is named. We sat together on his knee while he made a big fuss of us. My mother kept us beautifully dressed, and we really did have white fur coats and hats. I have a picture of us in them, though I don't know where we ever went to wear them.

Mother was the nearest thing our community had to a doctor. She had trained in England as a nurse under Edith Cavell, who was twelve years her senior. After graduation they became close friends as Mother went on to take a further year of obstetrics and become a District Nurse, working in the London slums as a midwife. They continued to correspond even after we came to Canada. I can remember many times in Clo'oose, men coming to the door in the dark of night, swinging lanterns and taking Mother away to look after their wives.

When I was five there were close to 25 children in the community, and a teacher was sent up from Victoria to operate the one-room school and board with whoever could have her. I remember one school Christmas party where there was a real live Jack-in-the-box in black tights, a little red coat, and a black stocking face. I'll never forget the screams that went up when he popped out, and I didn't know until it was time to go home that Jack was my petite mother.

By this time we also had what we grandly called The Hotel, or the Bungalow Inn, although it was nothing like the grand structure pictured in the West Coast Development Company brochures. In fact, it was not a hotel at all, but a large log cabin at the end of the beach. This was used for all sorts of social gatherings and fairs, where everyone would display his or her best efforts in cooking, sewing, or garden produce, and prizes were awarded.

The sea never lost its fascination for us. All kinds of things came ashore, especially after a storm. Perhaps it would be something from a wreck, or from Japanese fishermen, or it might be marine life. Once a fairly large whale was beached

Clo'oose bonfire

Surf of the Pacific at the Clo'oose hotel site

and we noticed it had two small, leg-like protuberances where hind legs might have been. Everyone in town gathered to see it, and a mysterious expert from Victoria with a long name even came up to have a look. Another day a baby seal came ashore. It was completely unafraid, and we children adored it. It arrived almost daily—our parents fed it, I guess—and we played with it for most of the summer. It would even go up on the porch of one of the houses behind the beach. In the fall it disappeared, but to our utter delight it was back the next summer, but that fall it took off, never to return.

Swimming was impossible and we were only allowed to go wading with adults around because of the very strong undertow along the beach, which we could feel dragging at our legs with every step. But we had lots of fun with the seaweed and kelp, putting it on each other's heads like hair, playing crack the whip and skipping with the kelp, and helping our parents drag some up to the cabins to fertilize the gardens.

Very little news of the outside world got through to us. Only very occasionally did we see a newspaper, and by then the news was often weeks or months old. The boat rarely called in winter, and Mother said that we didn't know there was a war on till the first boat arrived in the spring of 1915. As soon as they heard, most of the men, the government employees and some of the fishermen, left to join up. My father was among them.

Those who were left clung even more closely together and helped each other in every way possible. The Indians were not unfriendly, although they blamed the white man for bringing the storms which had wrecked their boats and nets, and at times they held very noisy gatherings.

We could hear them those nights, shouting and beating drums, which made us all uneasy. It was a hard time for everyone, and people began to leave as the West Coast Development Company's plans fell apart and the promised west coast road failed to materialize.

Then came the day my sister got meningitis. I will never forget my Mother sitting in a rocking chair with Marguerite on her lap, wrapped in a heavy blanket. The baby looked quite blue and was unconscious. Mother thought she had gone, and she cried, "Oh God, give me back my baby." She sobbed and sobbed while I huddled, petrified, in a corner. Suddenly Marguerite moved ever so slightly and Mother screamed joyfully, "She's alive, she's alive!"

Marguerite's recovery was slow, but as soon as Mother felt that she could travel, she hurried us down to Victoria, leaving everything. No more Clo'oose, alone, for Mother.

We got settled in Victoria, once again with our Welsh friends the Meredith-Joneses, who had left Clo'oose just ahead of us. Mother made one more trip back to collect her belongings, but found that vandals had done a lot of damage and little was left to salvage.

ANOTHER LAND DEVELOPMENT was attempted after World War I, when a promoter enticed British immigrants and prairie farmers to invest their life savings and move to Clo'oose where a grand hotel and a successful fish cannery were about to be established. At the height of this scheme, the white population rose to two hundred people, but the plan fell through when the Nitinat cannery failed in the 1920s. Many of the new settlers were upset by their

North end of Nitinat Lake

60-foot canoe on the shore of Nitinat Lake

Carmanah lighthouse

losses, and the promoter finally offered to buy them out...but his cheques bounced when they were taken back to civilization to be cashed. After that the community dwindled again, shrinking to around twenty people for many years until the town was officially abandoned in 1966.

A few years later my husband and I went back to Clo'oose to rekindle some of my memories. The summer resort hotel—the dream promised by the West Coast Development Company—was then a reality; a former settler, Dorothy Ordway, and her son, Jim Hamilton, had returned to Clo'oose and put their two homes to this use. We chartered a small Air West plane and landed on Nitinat Lake at Brown's Bay. Jim met us and took us by canoe out over the Bar and around to the mouth of the Cheewhat River, near his summer home.

I remembered Jim's mother well from my childhood, and she told me that she had often baby-sat me when she was a young girl. She said one of the first things Dad did when he arrived in 1911 was order rose bushes, and Dorothy present-ed me with a rosebush that was a descendant of his collection. She said that they had always called that bush after Dad.

Dorothy had become the postmistress for the few remaining settlers until the official demise of the village, and she was the custodian of the village's treasures. This included the official Honour Scroll of the men from Clo'oose who gave their lives in World War I. It was an awesome list from such a tiny community. Of thirty-one men who went overseas, eleven were killed. My father's name was on that list.

I was surprised at how accurate were my memories of where all the homes had been, but although I felt that I knew exactly where our cabin was, it was so overgrown that I was within a few yards of it before I found it. Only four logs remained standing, and after climbing inside all I could find was the cast-iron oven door to our stove.

During our trip we paid a visit to Carmanah lighthouse, hiking six miles along the beach and life-saving trail. On our way back the next day we suddenly realized that the tide had come in behind us and, to our horror, was rushing out again in front of us. We tried to find a way across, but the water was getting deeper every minute, so we just held hands tightly and walked right in. The drag on our legs was scary, but we made it.

And there wasn't a single footprint but ours all along that beautiful Clo'oose beach.

LUND
THE BEGINNING
OF THE ROAD

SHIRLEY CORBETT

LUND WAS FOUNDED by a Swedish pioneer who came to Canada because he heard that Canadians didn't have to work in the rain. This coast community has evolved and survived over the past 100 years, from the time when it was a winter camping ground for Salish Indians, through the boom years of logging and fishing, to its present status as service centre for tourists, and endpoint of the Sunshine Coast Highway, 28 kilometers northwest of Powell River.

"The best friend the native people ever had," is how the late Coast Salish Indian chief Bill Mitchell described Fredrick Gottfrid Thulin, the Swede who gave Lund, B.C., its name. Thulin's nickname, "Poppa," suggests he was a friend to everyone.

Fredrick was 13 and a farm worker in Sweden when his elder brother Charles emigrated to the United States. After a couple of false starts, Charles went to Winnipeg, Manitoba. Taking advantage of a free ride on the new railway, he travelled to the coast to help clean up after the 1886 fire which all but demolished Vancouver.

From Vancouver Charles moved to Pendrell Sound and began handlogging. It was here, in 1889, that 16-year-old Fredrick joined his brother. They logged for the rest of that year, skidding their timber into the salt water where it was boomed, towed to Vancouver, and sold at auction.

Most pioneers are somewhat visionary, and Fredrick was no exception. He soon owned a piece of land at Hole-in-the-Wall, on Malaspina Strait, but he was always on the lookout for a harbour where he could build a wharf. The natural harbour the brothers found in the Strait of Georgia, near the entrance to Desolation Sound, had been a Coast Salish winter campground for hundreds of years.

According to Bill Mitchell, the Salish had little huts all around the harbour, and lived at one side or the other, depending which side was most sheltered from the prevailing wind. They hunted and dug for clams and if there was enough food they stayed all winter.

Surrounded on three sides by rocky, fir-covered

City of Lund II *from side of* Admiral Evans, *March 20, 1920*

Second City of Lund, *about 1910. Fredrick is at far left.*

Original hotel, burned in a 1918 forest fire. Fredrick, left, by the horse. Charles is far right, holding the wing of an eagle.

cliffs sloping down to a natural basin, the inlet must have reminded the Thulins of a forest grove, because that is what "lund" means in Swedish. The word was short and easy to remember, so in 1890 the harbour was named.

There was a certain amount of traffic through the area, even then. Fishermen were constantly back and forth; tugs stopped every three or four weeks to leave mail and supplies for loggers coming down from the bush. The tugs anchored at a boomstick out in the harbour, and supplies were rowed ashore from there.

Eventually Fredrick and Charles built a wharf, using timbers 20 meters high for the front of the wharf, graduating to smaller logs at the back. The brothers worked long hours, cutting and installing logs in the day, weighing them down with rocks during low tides at night. They also built a little store, rowing the 85 nautical miles to Vancouver for supplies of flour, sugar, tea, and coffee.

In 1892 a post office was added to the store, and the Union Steamship line began making regular mail and provision trips. Two years later the Thulins built the first licensed hotel north of Vancouver. For those visitors taking too much advantage of the licensed premises, the astute Poppa built a little jail under the hotel where rowdies could be locked up overnight.

Within the next few years, Charles and Poppa cleared and drained the virgin land to convert it to farm land, devised a system for piping water from the creek to the wharf for sale to tugboats, and

built another store a few kilometers away at what is now the Sliammon reserve. Fredrick also made nets and fished for dogfish, rendering the livers into oil which was sold to loggers for 25 cents a gallon. The loggers used the oil on skidways to get their timber into the water.

In his spare time, Fredrick learned enough Salish to be able to communicate. But the man who taught him, Billy Pielle, had a stutter, so he sounded pretty funny when he spoke the language. Poppa also allowed the Indians to have a quiet drink in a back room of the hotel, since Indians were not allowed to drink in a public bar.

Logging and fishing were big business at that time, and it was not long before the brothers had built a tugboat and a larger hotel, the Malaspina, to accommodate the growing settlement and transient business. Until 1901, when the Thulins brought in the first donkey engine to be seen on this part of the coast, power was supplied by eight yoke of oxen, which were used for farming and hauling.

The brothers experienced their share of setbacks. The tug boat they designed and built in 1900, the *City of Lund*, was destroyed by fire a year later. Their second boat, the *Dolphin*, fared better, and they kept her until 1909 when she was sold, replaced by a bigger and better *City of Lund*. Perhaps the name was fated. While she was lying peacefully at anchor one night in 1920, she was rammed by a large passenger steamer, the *Admiral Evans*. The *City of Lund* sank within a few minutes, fortunately without loss of life. The first little hotel, along with several other buildings, was demolished in a 1918 forest fire; the Malaspina was saved.

When Charles and Poppa Thulin amicably dissolved their partnership in 1927, Charles went to live and work in a spot he had rejected years earlier as "no good"—Campbell River. He died there in 1932.

Fredrick had always been a soft touch for anyone needing a grubstake, and perhaps that is one of the reasons he became bankrupt several times. When his sons, Gerald and Holger, took over the business in 1934, a year before Poppa died, there wasn't much left but outstanding accounts, according to Ruby Thulin, Poppa's daughter-in-law.

Logging and fishing remained primary industries in Lund for many years, attracting other immigrants. One of these families was the Sorensens. Olga Sorensen, now 94 and living in Powell River, came to Lund from Denmark in 1923 with her two children, Jens, 9, and Lillie, 7. Her husband, Per, had arrived two years before and was working for the Thulins.

"Fred Thulin hired my husband as a gardener. Well, he was no gardener, he was a farmer, but one winter on the prairies [Manitoba] was enough for him and he was ready to take anything."

None of the family spoke English, although Per refused to use Danish more than necessary because he was afraid people would laugh at his country dialect. Jens and Lillie were refused admission at the little school until they learned their new language, but the teacher said they could attend recess to play with the other children.

"But that wasn't good enough. I knew my children had to have an education, so I told my husband to put his foot down with the teacher. I soon had my way."

Twenty years later, in 1943, Lillie was teaching at the same school that had once refused her admission.

The Sorensen's first home was a small house owned by the Thulins that Mrs. Sorensen says was haunted. "I used to wake up at night and feel that someone was standing by the bed laughing at me. One night something tugged at my nightgown. I thought I had caught it on a nail and bent down to look, but nothing was there."

Mrs. Sorensen learned that a sea captain had once lived in the house and, in a fit of temper, had thrown one of his many children down the stairs to its death. The ghosts did not frighten the family, and they stayed in the house for four years, until Poppa wanted more rent than they could afford to pay.

They moved into a huge building that had been erected as a cannery but never used. Per was no longer working for the Thulins, but had been logging and working on the mud road between Lund and Sliammon. Everything built by the settlers was built to last, and the mud road was no exception. It was not paved until 1954, signalling the end, two years later, of the 22-hour Vancouver to Lund steamship crossing.

Lund's social life in the depression was more lively than that enjoyed by the hamlet today. Until

Second hotel; the original hotel is to the right

(PABC #HP48390)

a community hall was built on land donated by Poppa, dances were held every couple of weeks in the hotel.

"Everyone used to walk in from outlying homes, bringing their children with them. A makeshift toilet and a huge bed for the children was set up at one end of the room. We had to dance until daybreak because we couldn't see to get home until then," Mrs. Sorensen remembers.

She also recalls many nights when the jail held a tenant, including one man who tried to frighten everyone by putting his head into the wood-burning stove.

"Every New Year's Day there was a huge, free party for the whole community, to celebrate Mr. Thulin's birthday. And during the week, someone always seemed to be having a coffee party."

Along with the Thulins and the community, the Sorensen family prospered. Per bought a ten-meter, Coast Salish dugout canoe for fishing trips. On the first family outing they rowed across the water to the "deep hole" off Savary Island, still a favoured fishing spot. "We rowed round and round that deep hole, and in half an hour Per had caught 28 fish. My husband said if it was that easy, that's how he was going to make his living." In 1927 Per became a commercial fisherman.

They outfitted the dugout with a noisy little Easthope motor that had one speed—fast. But that didn't prevent Per from trolling for salmon. To slow down he merely filled a canvas bag with rocks and towed it along behind. Because of the noise this motor made, the Sorensens christened their boat *Roaring Gimlet*.

Other boats were bought over the years, and Per often ferried visitors to the summer homes that were beginning to spring up on Savary. Today Per's grandson, Philip Russell, 38, ferries visitors and residents by means of the Lund water taxi.

Gradually the small community changed from a logging and fishing centre to a tourist spot. Independent loggers were bought out by larger companies; the fish-buying station was discontinued in 1981 since small catches made it impractical to maintain. The wharf built by the Thulins was partly demolished by a strong north-wester in 1954, and was replaced by a paved government wharf.

The fourth and present owners of the business started by Charles and Fredrick are Terry and Ewald Werner. With a staff of 25 to 50, depending on the season, they run the Lund Breakwater Inn, store, post office, and gas bar. The hotel looks, on the outside, just as it did in 1903 when it was built, although the inside has been damaged three times by fire.

Lund is still a community of about 300 people living in wooden houses strung around the harbour, perched on the hillsides, or hidden back in the bush. Until a couple of years ago, a number of colourful and innovative boat homes dotted the harbour, adding to the transient ambience of Lund. Without even the official designation "village," Lund is just part of electoral district A.

There is no longer a jail under the hotel, no oxen plod the paved roads, and a parking lot covers the old gardens. Yet Lund lives. For some it may be the end of the highway or a place to gas up the boat before heading into Desolation Sound, but residents see it in a different light. About four years ago, a new sign was erected at Lund, proudly proclaiming it to be the *beginning* of the road and the start of a 15,020 km drive that ends in Puerto Montt, Chile. And there will always be people like Philip Russell who stay on. These summers he is accompanied by the next generation of water taxi drivers, four-year-old Daniel and Stacey, two. They make a living in the summer and get by in the winter.

"I just wouldn't live anywhere else," he says.

Lund Harbour 1954

LOST VILLAGES
of Vancouver Island

JEAN WALLBANK

BEAVER COVE IS a calm and lovely harbour situated near the northeast end of Vancouver Island's rugged shoreline. It was named for the beavers that inhabited the flats of the Tsultan River, a tributary of the Kokish, that empties into the Cove. Years ago there were two communities snuggled into Beaver Cove's timbered shores, but in later years, when I made a sentimental journey to the scenes of my childhood, there was nothing left of either.

The first settlement in the Cove was built as a commercial venture by the Beaver Cove Lumber and Pulp Company in 1917. Built on the southern shore, the development was surprisingly large for the period. It included a 200-ton pulp mill, saw mill, shingle mill, and accommodations for 140 working men, with a townsite of about 20 houses. In addition, there was a Chinese settlement, a deep-sea wharf, and a hotel. This community was known as Beaver Cove.

The mill was in operation for a year, but a larger development was needed to supply logs. Some of the railroad was built for this purpose, but the company went bankrupt in 1920, and for many years it was in the hands of a caretaker, Leonard Frolander, who had been logging superintendent.

In 1925 a sawmill was built on the other side of the harbour by the firm of Wood and English. The mill, together with the logging terminus, formed a community known as Englewood. It was roughly the size of Beaver Cove, and included a fairly large number of Japanese who built their own bunk houses, cook house, and married quarters. Some of the mill employees lived in Beaver Cove, commuting each day by gas boat.

It was December 1929 when I first saw the Cove, and the great buildings of the old mill loomed dark and gaunt against the sky. The road ran from the wharf, where we disembarked from

Beaver Cove school, about 1930

the Union steamship, between these buildings to the mill pond. Here was a cluster of ten houses known as the lower townsite. The house that my father had rented was one of six identical houses built in a row. Each was composed of kitchen, living room, two bedrooms, and bathroom complete with plumbing. The homes in the lower townsite were lit with coal oil lamps or gasoline lanterns. The rooms were small and dark, and the lower half of each wall was wainscoting. No paint had been applied to the outside, and our house, at first sight, was not particularly inviting. With paint and paper my mother soon made the inside comfortable and hospitable, a place where young people gathered for evenings of fun with my two teenage sisters and brother.

From the windows we could see Mt. Wholesworth, a small mountain known as "the elephant." Its long slope towards the southeast resembled the trunk, and it was not hard to imagine that the two bumps to the right of it were the head and back.

From the lower townsite, the road sloped upward to another cluster of houses, the upper townsite. We were happy when, a year or two later, one of these houses became available to us, for they were larger, better built, and much in demand. Near them was the water wheel, which supplied electricity to this part of the community. The weather turned cold the December we arrived, and the water wheel came to a halt, spewing icicles until it had the appearance of a fairy palace of shining crystal. For most of the year, however, its soft purr mingled with the voice of the brook which tumbled down the hillside.

From the upper townsite you could follow the railroad grade to an old farm. This homestead was begun around the turn of the century by a man named Corney, a former sea captain. In 1929 Canadian Forest Products purchased this property and Captain Corney returned to England. I never knew the old gentleman, but I heard that he had a remarkable tom cat which attacked anyone who dared to trespass on his property!

My school friend, Annabel, lived there at one time. She and her younger brother walked a mile to school each morning. One day they were accosted by a cougar. With great presence of mind, Annabel hit it over the head with her lunch bucket, and the big cat ran off into the forest.

By the mid-thirties, the old farm had been deserted for a number of years, but it was much loved for its beauty and tranquillity. The huge blackberry patch supplied the whole community with a bountiful crop every summer. In April the clearing was singing with bird calls and perfumed with blossoms. We loved to gather daffodils and narcissi that had grown wild in the grassland, and when we approached very quietly, we sometimes saw a black bear sleeping in the sun, or a herd of elk slipping into the shadows.

Deepsea wharf at Beaver Cove, where Union steamships tied up

Beaver Cove pulp mill, about 1936

Englewood sawmill, 1929

There was another field near the upper townsite known as Piggery Park. If, as seems likely, it was once a home for pigs, they had been removed long before I arrived at the Cove, for the clearing then had a thick covering of grass and was edged with shade trees, the latter dearly loved by spectators of the annual school picnic.

We had various forms of entertainment in those days when television was unknown. During the summer we went hiking or boating and usually ended up with a community campfire in the evening. Everyone, young and old, attended the campfire. Guitars and harmonicas provided us with music, and everyone joined in the singing. Sometimes we played games, and we always buried potatoes in the hot coals, digging them out later to peel and devour. Nothing since has tasted so good as that combination of potato, salt, and wood ash.

Our favourite place for swimming was at the junction of the Kokish and Tsultan Rivers, known to us as the "Deep Hole." During my visit, this was the only untouched spot that I found. It looked exactly as I remembered it.

Like all young people, we had our parties. These were held in our homes or even in an empty house if the weather was warm. We danced waltzes and foxtrots to records played on an old, wind-up gramophone. "Three Little Words," "Little White Lies," "Isle of Capri," and "Honeymoon Hotel" were among the tunes popular at that time.

Once in a while we arranged a more formal dance, using, for this purpose, the big dining room and kitchen in the hotel. Refreshments were donated by the residents of the Cove, and Mrs. George McLean generously supplied both the piano and her services as pianist. Her son Hugh played the violin. Sometimes we were lucky enough to get an Indian by the name of Gideon who played the saxophone remarkably well. People came from miles around; even small babies attended the dances, for often there was no one at home to take care of them. The older children always hoped they could stay awake long enough to partake of the refreshments.

During the thirties, the ocean was our only highway and the arrival of any ship was an event no one wanted to miss. Twice weekly we congregated on the wharf to greet the *Catala* or *Cardena*, the Union steamships that brought mail, supplies, and passengers. The mission hospital ship, *Columbia*, called at the Cove occasionally, as did the *Sky Pilot*. When the latter was in port we had church services in the school house.

A company house in the upper townsite had been converted for the school. It was an arrangement of one large room in which eight grades were taught. Except for a sink in the cloakroom, the plumbing had been removed, necessitating the building of an outhouse at the back.

Our nearest shopping centre was Alert Bay on Cormorant Island, some seven miles distant and perhaps an hour's run from the Cove. There was

Englewood, 1926

(PABC #HP67963)

also a boat called the *Jolly Jumbo* which cruised along the coast during the summer months. She was a fair-sized yacht, and her owner, a Mr. Whitehead, carried a tempting array of clothing, toys, household supplies, and bric-a-brac. This floating department store was welcomed in all the lonely corners of the coast by people who seldom made a trip to the city.

At one time, Mr. Whitehead had on board a small beauty salon, equipped with a permanent wave machine. There, on a sweltering day in August, I had my first permanent, sitting quietly, if a trifle apprehensively, while the beautician attached the machine to each carefully wound strand of hair. When she had finished, I looked as though I were about to be devoured by an octopus. Then there was an anxious moment when the electricity was turned on, my scalp began to tingle, and I was sure I would be burned. The heat of the machine, added to the heat of the day and the discomfort of holding up the heavy curlers, gave me a raging headache, but I left the yacht feeling that this was a small price to pay for curly hair!

ALL THIS WAS the Beaver Cove of the past, a place of long, lovely trails down which Annabel and I wandered on warm summer evenings in search of the cows, leisurely eating salmonberries on the way. The Beaver Cove of today is literally a different one.

Before Canadian Forest Products erected the present terminus, they completely destroyed the old. Every building was torn down or moved, and the very topography was changed as hills were leveled and streams diverted. On this new site, in 1956, they began construction of a beach camp as part of their multi-million dollar development, building a network of truck roads and railroads, and also a new camp at an elevation of 400 feet which they named Kokish.

At the time of my visit, there was an excellent highway joining the community with northern points, and a government ferry service to Kelsey Bay provided a link with the Island Highway to the south. Today a new highway has made the ferry service obsolete.

Across the bay from Beaver Cove, the community that was Englewood is completely gone, and in its place is a growth of alders. After the mill was dismantled and removed, the houses became a liability, and fire was used as a clean, thorough method of destroying them.

I had lived there, too, in its heyday, when my father was employed at the mill as electrician. I attended school, and in the hall above the company office, parents and friends gathered to watch the annual school Christmas concert. On one of those occasions I sang a duet with Nora, a friend from Englewood school.

Life in Englewood was a little different from life in Beaver Cove, although both had the ever-present noise of the mill and the shriek of the whistle which announced shift changes. Englewood also had several feet of sawdust in the soil, and a great deal of ash from the burner fell regularly on the Monday wash. Also disappointing was the water supply, which was the colour of tea — although it seemed to have no ill effects on our health. The water at the Cove was clear, untainted, and delicious.

The people of the two communities did not intermingle a great deal. As a child, while living in one place, I rarely went to the other. It was mostly a matter of transportation, for a boat was needed to cross the bay.

My return to Englewood brought back nostalgic memories. I stood under the alders during my visit and remembered the whine of the saws and the chunking of the chain that dumped refuse into the burner. I thought of the huge freighters that had called in to load lumber, the house which had been home, and the board walk down which Nora and I coasted our sleigh one winter evening, to land in a snowdrift at the bottom, helpless with laughter.

The ashes underfoot were deep and black. These and a piece of twisted trestle were all that remained.

I talked to a few people of the changes that had been made. The young woman at the ferry wharf looked bewildered.

"Changes?" she said. "Why, I grew up around here and it has always been just like this!"

I knew then that the villages of my childhood were, indeed, lost villages.

Anne CAMERON

Kyuquot Forest Protectorate

There are trees here stand barkless
their weathered gray exposed wood
twisted and turned upon itself
like a corkscrew, and you know
only the roots sunk deep in the
rocky earth kept these trees from
spiralling away, spinning forever
toward nothing, like those timidly
smiling men with empty faces
who never learned to settle for
any one thing, any one person

Here you learn to be content
with nothing, here you can learn
to exist with sorrow, you can come
face to face with what you have lost
and know keeping something is impossible

The Indians here have eyes like mourners
and their smiles only play at the
edges of their lives, until you feel
they are waiting, and you wonder
                    For What

And sometimes the wind screams at you
days and days of lunatic whining
coming from the mountains and pleading
teasing at your skull, piercing your ears,
winding in and out between your teeth,
until you feel yourself twisting, twisting
like a corkscrew, spinning, spinning
and your roots not yet sunk deep
into the chilling rock soil

Hecate

cement forms
derelict in the water
huge metal vats
unused and rusting
houses
empty houses
floors tilted
stairways
staggering
windows
like eyeless holes
in a bleached
    skull
I walked in the lupine field
picked blackberries
wondered if the bear who left
his droppings
would return
and reclaim his bush
feeling
eyes
from the forest
eyes
from inside the
empty houses
eyes
slanted
and dead
staring
and I panicked

MINSTREL ISLAND

HOWARD WHITE

CORDERO CHANNEL LEADS THE small boater north from the Yaculta rapids. On this day the water was very blue. On the near side, toward a row of bluffs I recognized from dreams, it got greener, then black. I wondered why those bluffs made such an impression on me. They weren't the highest I'd seen. Maybe the bluffest. They hung over the channel just north of Shoal Bay, dusted lime green and peach, and scarlet from lichen. I swung over so close you could reach out and touch the rock wall and catch hold of outleaning bushes. Mary was alarmed to be running at full speed so close to shore, and I laughed at her worry.

Signs of abandoned logging caught my eye on both sides of the channel. On the far side, where last time through I saw an old ruined camp with grey cookhouse collapsed at one end, still standing at the other, there was now a new camp with white mobiles and fresh brown logs. The steep sidehills were etched with the wavery lines of old cat roads angling steeply toward the beach. I thought of the trip I'd taken around Nelson Island with my dad the year previous. Looking up at lines like these, Dad had said, "It hurts me to look at those roads, clawed into the rock with little old cats, every half

mile another one that some poor bloody fool put the best years of his life into."

His sympathy was more perfect for having spent the best years of his life doing just that himself.

I HAD GROWN UP IN the last days of the old coast when every bay had a gyppo booming logs and life followed the cycle of the weekly steamer call, but it had never seemed special to me then. It had seemed a half-existence outside the real march of the twentieth century, a backwater my whole growing-up was aimed at escaping. It wasn't until I did escape, and spent a harrowing decade in the city discovering what a half-existence really was, that the coast began to take on this golden glow, a place of legend. It was a glow that seemed to be recognized nowhere in the country's official culture so in 1972 I started *Raincoast Chronicles* to rescue the coast from oblivion. But after two years devoted to extolling that quality without actually seeing proof, I was beginning to grow weary of the sound of my own voice trying to convince myself. I hated myself every time I used the word "legend."

Mary, my partner in this quest for the holy grail

of regional character, had never believed it in the first place and suffered less from doubt. She had been captivated by the sheer novelty of publishing a magazine, but that was wearing down, too. The spaces between issues were getting bigger.

I don't suppose I confided any of this doubt to Joe Simson, because we didn't talk about things like that. Joe was a history buff. His "pappy," as he said, had been postmaster of the village of Granville and one of the elders of the Vancouver business community, and in his declining years Joe had devoted himself to remembering his beginnings. When our first issue appeared he had sent us a letter containing several corrections penciled in large printing on lined paper torn from a scribbler, and a cheque for a hundred dollars. As we kept on, the notes kept on, along with the cheques. One day he drove into our yard in his jeep, a lean, handsome man of 74 with curly white hair and glasses that made his eyes appear monstrous.

"You're not getting out enough," he told us gruffly, looking around at our cramped pink house-trailer with its black soot-stains. "You better take my boat and get out and see some of this stuff you're writing about."

I am sure if it had been put to us any other way by anyone else, we would have said we were too busy working on the next issue. But we had come to think of Joe as our patron saint, and he was serious about this. Besides, Joe's boat was gorgeous.

The *Beaver V* was a 30-foot double-ender powered by a 10-14 Easthope. It had been built in 1948 and Joe bought it from a fisherman in Secret Cove, moving the motor back into the fish hold to make more room inside. It was a classic one-man troller, one of the last around, and certainly the best preserved, with one of the very last operating Easthope motors. Everything was heavy-duty, newly painted and in perfect working order. It was the ideal vessel in which to go searching for the lost soul of the coast.

We had no actual plans. Joe had said, "Stop in and see Olaf Hansen in Port Neville, why don't you?" and that had established an unconscious goal in my mind, but I wasn't getting too set on it. In the geography of the world that existed inside my mind, Port Neville was a long way away. It was "up north." Among my current friends, more had been to Paris than to Port Neville. But Joe seemed to think it was in our range. I had mentioned Minstrel Island, and he didn't even seem to think that was out of the question.

Since becoming a half-assed historian of the coast, Minstrel Island had loomed ever larger in my mind. From the turn of the century on it seemed to serve as a nerve centre of the logger's universe, the Dodge City of their wild west. For me it would be like a pilgrimage to Mecca, but I would be satisfied with less, if only I could

recapture some of that shivery old feeling about the mystery and wonder of the coast to recharge my mythic batteries.

We spent a night at the site of Dad's old logging camp in Green Bay. The main bay where the bunkhouses had been was seamless forest down to the water, and you could barely even find where our old log dump had been blasted into the sidehill. I shut off the engine and tried to commune, but the place did nothing for me. I wondered if it was me, the place, or the time of day. Morning was always best for feeling a place. But I didn't want to hang around down here where I'd been before. I wanted to plunge northward, to some of these places I'd heard of all my life but never seen: Von Donop Inlet, the Yacultas, Hole-in-the Wall, Blind Channel, Loughborough Inlet, Forward Harbour, Topaz Harbour, Knight Inlet. New and strange places were the surest way to strip away the numb crust and bare the feeling stuff.

We tried to put in the next night at Redonda Bay on Big Redonda Island. In the twenties Redonda Bay, then called Deceit Bay, had been big doin's, with a railroad camp, a shingle mill, a cannery, and a store that supplied a galaxy of little camps up Toba, Bute and Ramsay Arm. Deceit Bay was full of wonders in those days. The logs were brought down the steep slope to the salt-chuck by means of a funicular railroad, and the bay was dominated by a big steamer which was pulled up on shore between the various buildings. This was the SS *Transfer*, a 122-foot paddle-wheeler originally built in 1893 for Captain Irving, who had it in service on the lower Fraser River for a good many years. In its final resting place its staterooms housed an army of Chinese workers while its boiler supplied steam to drive the mill and cannery. Electric lights blazed all through the night, a rare thing on the coast of those days. I had built up quite a romantic idea of this place in my mind, and was very keen to stop the night to look for traces of past glory, but my hopes were soon dispelled. Rounding the point we were confronted by a large sign ordering us to turn back. Redonda Bay was now the site of a wilderness prison camp and strictly off limits to anyone who wasn't a criminal. But even from a distance I could see there was no trace of the old town remaining, only a white quadrangle of mobile bunkhouses. We went on to Churchhouse for the night, and got up early to catch slack water at the Yaculta and Green Point rapids.

As we passed north of the rapids we began to notice a change in the type of boats we encountered. Closer to the populated centres they had been predominantly smaller pleasure craft, mostly Canadian, but now they were mostly American and large. They would swerve off their courses and come close as they passed, admiring our authenticity as their wash made like to end us. We glowered and refused to return their friendly waves until the burden of so much disapproval began to weigh us down. We began waving back, but lifelessly.

Working our way up Sunderland into the main stream of Johnstone Strait, we found the seas increasing. If the *Beaver V* hadn't been so good in head seas I might have started to worry, and thought of heading back to Forward Harbour. But the *Beaver* was showing she was made for it and threw herself across each succeeding swell with a will, so I kept her heading into it.

It was the wrong thing to do. We didn't know it because we hadn't turned on the radio for two days, but there was a gale warning out. We didn't see another boat for hours. They were all tied up waiting for it to blow through. By the time we were looking up the broad freeway of Johnstone Strait, the swells were as wide across their backs as the boat was long, and things were starting to crash around with the force that breaks. The water was black with wind, and standing at the wheel back of the wheelhouse the spray was whipping me in the face until I had given up feeling salty and rugged and started to admit to myself I had taken about as much as I could stand. But there was nowhere to get out of it on the *Beaver*.

I kept on, searching every wave for a chunk that could put out our prop or a deadhead that would smash out the bottom before we could get into the skiff. There are just as many chunks in rough water as calm, I told myself, you just couldn't see them. The late sun turned the surface of the waves into glittering gold foil. Between blinding flashes my eyes would see green and black voids full of chimerical deadheads. I waited for every pulse of the engine with arrested heartbeat.

Within a few minutes of turning into Port Neville the water was calm and full of American yachts, all amazed to see us materialize out of the storm. I admitted it was a touch lumpy out. We found Olaf Hansen, but didn't get much out of him. Some of the biggest names in the publishing game had been in to get his story, and we didn't really rate.

Johnstone Strait was flat as glass when we got back out on it the next day. The motor seemed to have recovered its health and popped us along the five miles to Havannah Channel and Minstrel Island country in 45 minutes.

When I'd come through before with John Daly, a fisherman from Pender Harbour, we stopped in Port Harvey to see an old gyppo logger named Dick Donovan. His camp was only a few minutes away now and I had it in mind to drop in on him, but before I could well see the outline of his bunkhouse I could tell things had changed. There was a huge tent of orange plastic hulking in the woods behind the house, big enough to house a forty-foot sailboat, which I had no doubt it

actually did. When you see a shed like that on this coast, it only means one thing. Donovan's boat was still there so I thought he might be too, but no such luck. The camp had been taken over by a family of you-alls named McAllister, and the boat they were building was amazing: a good forty feet, maybe more, with funny sharp points at both ends, and welded up out of steel. Dick Donovan was logging down at Pitt Lake, and they were renting the place.

I asked them about the bay we were in, Port Harvey, and found they already knew a lot of its history. Until the First World War there had been a settlement here called Cracroft, with a beer parlour and store, and it had rivalled Minstrel Island like Cimarron rivalled Dodge City. In *Woodsmen of the West*, M.A. Grainger's 1903 novel that was for me the Bible of the wild west coast, Cracroft was referred to as Port Browning, and one afternoon the hero left the beer parlour at Minstrel Island, which Grainger called Hanson Island, crossed the Blowhole in a rowboat and followed a path down Cracroft Inlet to the Cracroft beer parlour. Cracroft Inlet, a narrow, mud-choked gut that divided West from East Cracroft Island, ran right past Donovan's property.

The old Cracroft beer parlour had been a large frame building built on a flat rock just above the saltchuck. Grainger passed a happy evening there listening to a fiddler accompanied by another man who tapped on the fiddle strings with chopsticks. The barroom was crowded full, with men sitting all around the walls on chairs and benches and standing at the bar two rows deep, and a few moments after his arrival there was an eruption of shouting voices, followed by a short, sharp fight and a long, slowly subsiding growl of argument. The noisiest man in the bar was a hulking young American hobo who did an unsteady clog-dance bawling, "I'm a bobcat with tousels in me ears." Some nights before, Andre the Frenchman had stomped on the hobo's face in his caulk boots, leaving it hideously disfigured. When Grainger asked some men why they didn't stop the maiming, they looked thoughtful and said, "Well, maybe Andre had something against him." Like most of the buildings in logger country, the floors of the Cracroft Hotel were pocked and splintered from the spikes in loggers' caulk boots. But the Cracroft Hotel, if you looked closely, also had boot-pocks in an unusual place: on the barroom wall. The story behind this unnatural wonder has been told so many times it has come to rank as one of the legends of the coast.

Port Harvey at that time was quite a handlogging centre, and when these solitary, independent and agile men took a break from their brutal struggle with the sidehills, they tended to overcompensate. On this historic evening they had settled upon the pastime of dashing against the wall to see how high they could run up it in their caulk boots. The trick was to beat the last climber's height, but at all costs land on your feet when finished. If you fell, the next round was on you. The owner, Charlie Cavanaugh, measured the amount of beer he was selling against the damage to his wall and decided to cut the boys off. They protested without effect, then huddled down at their rowboats, and came back with a dozen screw jacks, the tools of the handlogger's trade, which they jammed under the uphill side of the building and began screwing. The pub creaked, seams popped, and it teetered precariously over the chuck. Cavanaugh rapidly recalculated his position and reopened the bar.

I'd heard this story from someone else, and told it to the McAllisters. They betrayed no sign they'd heard it until I was almost finished, then chimed in in unison to beat me to the ending. I felt like a fool, naturally, but they didn't seem to mind. Usually when you stopped at these little isolated places the people were so glad of fresh conversation they greeted you like royalty, but here they seemed tense and impatient. The kids looked bored and wandered off. The wife seemed impatient as well, although the man tried to make up for the rest. He started telling us a story about the old Cracroft storekeeper, but she wasn't satisfied by the way he went about it and took over. This storekeeper was also the postmaster apparently, and whenever a local woman sent in a mail order to Woodward's, he would open the envelope and cross off any items which could be purchased from him. Mrs. McAllister said they'd learned all about the place from some former resident who had written them a long, fine-print letter. The idea of a good local history source excited me, so I asked for the name. They didn't have it. Mrs. McAllister had burned the letter. She wasn't sorry.

"She wanted to correspond but I didn't," she said flatly. None of them seemed to care much about the history around them. I asked if there were many oldtimers around I could interview.

"Shoore, I think you oughta stop and see old Mackay. He's a real oldtime handlogger. Bit of a character, but he's been around here fer a coon's age. You'll see him going inta Minstrel, on the side there. Bright orange boat."

"And Hadley. There's an old Mr. Hadley and a young. Yew want the old. Git out in the channel agin and it's jist a cattywampus crost th bay. You'll see it. A real fine old feller."

THERE WAS NOW NOTHING to stop us so we set out for Minstrel Island, which was five miles away. Chatham Channel looked like a horror on the chart, with rocks all over and a five-knot current, but it turned out to be simple if you used the range markers. A straight, narrow alleyway, hills shaven, the odd tall tree here and there, then more green fuzz like a bad crewcut.

About halfway down I saw the orange boat that must have belonged to one of the other oldtimers McAllister told us about. It was tied up to a float shack on the north side. Opposite, on the south hillside, I saw signs of fairly recent disturbance, small alder and a gouge in the earth running up the vertical hillside to a standing wooden spar. It was the first wooden spar I'd seen since I was a kid. I was tickled. It even seemed to be rigged, although it looked so old I doubted it was in operation. On the beach below it was a tangle of logs and busted chunks, which I decided were the remains of a chute which slid down the hill, because they were all grey with age. I was tempted to go over, but the object of our journey beckoned at the end of the channel.

Minstrel looked like it should, I thought. Stuck to the backside of a steep little island, a small batch of buildings and floats, old. Musty, mildewy, in dank shade on a sunny afternoon, a long pier on pilings and a quadrangle of new government floats clustered with American yachts. The most active building was the store, built over the water on pilings like a cannery and parallel to the pier, a rambling cluster of tin-roofed sheds with little window panes. Inside, the floor was eroded by caulk boots at all the busy intersections, most deeply dished in front of the cash register where generations of Swede fallers had stood shuffling their spiked feet as they bought their Copenhagen snoose. Stock included nails, anchor chain, batteries, charts, galvanized buckets, frozen herring, minibikes, pennants, hardhats, plastic totem poles, Sportyaks, soup, nuts, bolts and groceries at twice normal prices. The owner was a stiff, hard-mouthed man very much not a part of the local scene who said ninety percent of the trade was to tourists, and was thinking of closing during the next winter except on mail days. When I put a few leading questions about the past, he made it clear he wasn't interested. There were hardly any loggers left, and he thought it was a good thing. His wife was fighting middle age with eye shadow and a tight sweater, flirty at the cash register.

It was a shallow bay with a sparse few houses to the left of the wharf and a few to the right, hugging the tideline and connected by a long footbridge with red government railings. Ashore there were two large buildings, either of which might have been the hotel. The one nearest the water was a bit smaller, a long narrow public structure of some kind with rows of small windows on two floors with more in the steep gables. There was something funny about its being so close to the beach, almost like somebody had started to drag it into the water and quit halfway. It was hard to imagine anyone building such an ambitious structure so uncomfortably close to the waterline. I could see a pool table through a ground floor window. The other building was bigger and stood on higher ground, a sagging three-storey barn with steep moss-laden roof, the walls a moth-eaten grey stained with green mold, almost invisible against the forest that reared up behind, dwarfing the settlement. Looking closely at the wall above the long enclosed porch, I detected faded lettering, "Hotel."

So this was the Minstrel Island Hotel, one of the holiest shrines of logging history. This was where Grainger stayed in 1907, paying for his patch of bare floor in the attic by sawing firewood for the kitchen. Every serious logger between 1900 and 1960 had a story to tell about the Minstrel beer parlour, but now I couldn't tell if it was even in use. It had a dead look. The grass was six inches high between the planks of the boardwalk. I dragged Mary up to the door and tried it. It opened.

The first thing that hit us, since the light was too dim to see anything, was the smell. It wasn't a bad smell, but a distinctive one. It was the smell of a logging camp bunkhouse. It's special, and you could guess some of the components: spilled beer, tobacco, unbathed bodies, laundry that's dirty with sawdust and pitch, drying boot-leather, grey army blankets, straw mattresses. You expect to find it in a bunkhouse and don't notice it. But finding it somewhere else, you pause to think what it is. The only non-bunkhouse I ever smelled it in was a little shack in Gibsons where a logger friend of ours lived between stints at camp, reproducing the bunkhouse lifestyle so precisely at home he was able to duplicate the scent that went along with it.

"Jesus, it smells exactly like Pete's," Mary said. It was hard to say why based on the present occupants—a pair of uncomfortable tourists sitting by a window and a couple of young guys lounging at a table with their legs hooked over chairs; they looked too quick to be local but seemed to know everyone. No logger in sight, but so many had bedded down in this building over the years their scent must have permeated the timbers. I was as uncomfortable as the tourists. There was no sense of public about the room. It was like we walked into someone's private home. Since we came in, the few other customers had been sneaking looks at us over their beer, but nobody made the faintest outward sign of wanting to serve us. There was a bar, but it had nothing on it, no taps, no fridge behind it, no sink. It didn't look like a beer had passed over it that year. The other tables had a few bottles though, and they got them somewhere. Maybe it's self-serve, I thought. Hell, maybe it's BYOB. Finally a very tired-looking woman dressed in a floppy, shapeless sweater appeared through a dark doorway, dragged herself to the bar and served us a couple of warm Lucky Lagers.

A radiophone blurted into life in some back room, Campbell River calling Minstrel Island, Campbell River calling Minstrel Island, Campbell River calling Minstrel Island and she dragged herself away to answer: Yeah, Minstrel here. I took the opportunity to snoop around. Behind the bar was a crooked little room littered with ripped-open beer cases in front of a bulky white

Minstrel Island

household fridge. An adjoining room was empty of tables, the floor rain-warped and in the middle a battery on charge. For some reason I was sure this was the room in which Grainger saw all the passed-out drunks stacked up like cordwood.

Looking over the railing on the way down the dock, we noticed something funny about the mudflat underneath. It had a peculiar texture to it, as if it was pebbled with stones under the film of mud, but it wasn't stones, it was bottles. Hundreds, thousands of bottles, covering the entire acre or so beside the wharf. I had never seen so many bottles anywhere in my life. We went back to the shore end of the dock and walked down onto the mudflat. Barnacled, broken, weedy, the bottle shards seemed as numerous as the stars in the sky, ones below filling the gaps between the ones above. They were all old. Tall beer bottles, Kik Cola, the brown ringed ones with Orange Crush in an orange diamond, unheard of whisky brands and one rusty caulk boot.

My old friend J.I. Rost, who has been cruising up and down the coast keeping an eye on things since 1928, points out that the bottles at Minstrel are one of the mysteries of the coast. Why are they there? You don't see them in other harbours—Gibsons, Heriot Bay, Irvine's Landing, Shoal Bay... Perhaps because there is practically nowhere to stand on Minstrel except the dock, the heavy drinkers favoured it as a location for their work. Or perhaps it was the only place on the coast where there was a large population of bottle-tossing drinkers but no commensurate population of local kids to collect empties the morning after.

Pondering the matter in the murk under the pier, I realized that for all I had heard about Minstrel I knew virtually nothing about the place. I decided to go find the two oldtimers McAllister had told us about, and do some research. I had seen some buildings at the downstream end of Chatham Channel on our way up, which I figured must be the oldtimer he said was just a "cattywampus" across the bay. We headed there first, figuring we could tie up for the night if all went well.

It was quite a scene. There were two big old dormer-roofed houses hunching over this pocket-sized cove, and at the water's edge a couple of large sheds. Beside them was a heavy-duty marine ways, and on the ways two new fifty-foot seine boats. A fancy floating motorhome was tied up along with several speedboats, a couple of small tugs and boomboats, two new aluminum gilnetters, and a small barge loaded with cedar shakes. There was a good deal of rusty equipment lying around, and a diesel lightplant was ratta-tat-tatting away somewhere out of sight. There were people moving around here and there. Young people. I'd never heard of this place before, but it was well and away the most lively and active spot

we'd stopped at. Hadley Bay. It was named that after the Hadleys, two generations of them; Merle the father and Bill the son.

Hadley senior was responsible for the bargeload of shakes, which we tried to tie beside. A short guy with curly hair and the look of a radio evangelist came bouncing out of a little day-cruiser to warn us off, saying the freighter would be coming to unload the barge during the night. Otherwise he was friendly and helped us pull the boat to a safe spot. Days later the bargeload of shakes was still waiting.

The bouncy guy was an American from Oregon who spent his holidays in Hadley Bay hanging out. He was in love with the old cattywampus and followed him around helping split shakes. As he explained it, old Merle was "just a fine human being to be around." When I told him I wanted to do an historical interview with his mentor, he was all for it and took me up to the older of the two houses.

Merle Hadley was a very pleasant, soft-voiced man probably somewhere in his late sixties. He seemed at peace with life. His corner was in order. His house had an air of well-worn comfort, and he and his wife both spoke as though they just couldn't imagine being anywhere or anybody else than they were. A shy man, he was a bit taken aback at being interviewed for publication, but he wasn't refusing. We sat at the kitchen table.

"Well let's see, my first trip up here was in 1925." He had a better drawl than McAllister. Nine-teen twen-ty *fiiivvvve*...Everything was in this slow drawly singsong. It was lovely. You just held your breath waiting to hear more.

In Pender Harbour we tended to mark off the historical periods by the various storekeepers who held sway, like English kings. "That was when Royal Murdoch had the store, or was it Jim Pope...?" Around Minstrel they tended to go by owners of the hotel.

"The one that owned it when I first came was Neil Hood. Evidently he'd got it quite cheap, you know, and it wasn't payin', then he built it up." The big long building with the pool table, I now discovered, was the former Cracroft Hotel, which had been towed around from Port Harvey on floats.

"Neil Hood done that. B'cause he was afraid that it would get big agen, there was so many tugboats over there. Evidently, if they could get a liquor licence, well any place'll boom.

"Taki had two loggers movin' floats, and they put that buildin' on the two big floats and moved it around. Set it right alongside of the wharf."

Hood's strategy worked a little too well. Soon he was making more money than he wanted.

"He didn't like payin' income tax. After five thousand you had to pay income tax, and after only about three months, he'd be up there. When he felt like it, he'd sell you a beer, but a lot of times he didn't feel like it. They'd come to the door—'Could I have a—' Slam! That was that. He'd wouldn't even let 'em get the words out of their mouth."

I pressed him for more Minstrel history, but having lived beside it for fifty years, he couldn't think of anything much to say about the place. They had a murder there one time...

"Tell me about that," I said.

"Well, I don't even know the fellow's name that was murdered. A fisherman though. He had, they figure, about seven hundred dollars in his pocket, and he was flashin' it around, you know. The last he was seen, he went up and he'd got a case a' beer. The next thing, they saw this blood at the corner of the little freight shed, and then the ramp comes down, and the blood started there and it come all the way down and it crossed two boats. The boat he was put on went.

"But the goll-darn body drifted right back t' Minstrel the next day. Right into the wharf. The Murphy kid, he had little raft there with a little outboard on it and he run right into it.

"When would that be? Oh, let me see... There was quite a bit of activity at Minstrel then. Port MacNeill Loggin' was goin' full blast. Bill and Sid were goin' over there t' school. Early fifties, maybe? I can't say.

"Scope, the policeman, knew it was an Indian boat, the third one out. They found a piece a' pipe they figured was what done the job. This boat went to Alert Bay directly from Minstrel and dumped the body offa Bones Bay. They went to Alert Bay and this woman said that somebody had drowned at Minstrel Island. But the body hadn't got back yet. Nobody else knew it. So it was a dead giveaway right there.

"But both those Indians committed suicide. The police was questioning 'em and they knew they was goina be caught. One a' them just gassed himself. And the other one jumped overboard. One was Pugels. Hmmm... what the heck was the other one? I don't know. They were from Village Island.

"There was more murders, but I can't think of 'em. There was one fella, I guess he went out of his mind or somethin', and he went and jumped overboard. There was always a lot of 'em hangin' around the wharf, leanin' on the rail waitin' for the steamer and partyin' on boats and what not, well, they saw it an' they pulled 'im back out. He got madder'n sam hell, 'e didn't wanta live, and so 'e jumped overboard again.

"They left 'im.

"Rita Wilson was just a young girl then and she was walkin' up these floats and right in b'tween the two floats was one a' these fellas y' know, his hair was all out like seaweed and she jis' screamed murder. I ferget if this was the same fella or another one. That Union boat, you know, when it went astern it sucked in anything that was out

there and it used to run the bodies right up on the beach.

"Oh we had rare times, alright."

I wish I could write how he pronounced those words: ray-er ty-eems. In that waltzing way. Even his wife laughed.

"When Neil Hood sold out, things started to go ahead. Izzy the Jew got it and he was trying to sell all the beer he could. In fact it was rumoured that he sold more beer in that hotel than all the rest of B.C. put together."

"That's a lot of beer," I said.

"Oh, a lotta beer. There was so many big camps in here."

Mrs. Hadley took it upon herself to lean toward me and whisper, "He means it was the highest selling *beer parlour* in B.C."

He wasn't sure of the hotel's line of succession after Izzy. I wanted to know Izzy's full name, but he didn't know it. He said nobody ever called him anything but Izzy the Jew.

"How many owners sence that—waall, it was changin' hands one night after another." The current owner was a man named Pearly Sherdal, a logger from the area. Pearly was a throwback, the last of the untamed bush apes. Everybody knew the story of how he came to own the pub. We'd already heard it three times. It went like this:

The manager had got tired of throwing him out for fighting and jumping up on tables in caulk boots and whatnot—throwing empty glasses out the window without opening it, or worse: singing. Singing was the baddest thing you could do under the old pub rules, and warranted instant chucking out. The rationale seemed to be, "once they start singing, who knows what they might do next...?" Pearly wasn't easy to chuck out, being 250 pounds or so of gristle and beergut, so the hotel manager barred him. Pearly ignored the bar, so the manager got an order from the police. To Pearly, of course, this was a totally unwarranted response to what he considered normal civilized behaviour, and he was indignant.

An old-time bush ape doesn't just get indignant to no purpose; he takes action on it. Pearly galloped down the wharf to where the weekly steamer was just that minute pulling out, took a flying leap onto the deck, and went all the way into Vancouver. Pearly had money, and when he got to town he had no trouble making a deal. A few days later he came back, walked up the wharf, rounded up everybody in town for a drink on the house, and strode into the hotel. The manager of course refused his order and told Pearly unless he left the building immediately he was going to have him placed under arrest.

Pearly no doubt milked the situation for everything it was worth before revealing he'd bought the hotel and legally pitching the manager through the door. You can imagine him putting on his look of false innocence: "Now Henry, don't you want to think about this for a minute? Why don't you just fetch us all a drink and tell me again why it is I'm not fit to drink in this beer parlour?" They say Pearly never did pay his back wages. The whole story sounded suspiciously apocryphal but everyone swore it was true, including Hadley. The hotel had been run ever since by Pearly's wife, Jean. It was her who'd served us the warm Lucky Lagers.

Pearly was Minstrel's favourite character. Even Hadley, who had the small towner's lack of generosity toward anyone who didn't fit in by local standards, had full admiration for Pearly.

"He's a great guy, you know. Around Minstrel when he's corned he always gets on this thing, he's goina "clean this place up." He'd pile all the beer cases in the middle of the wharf and set fire to 'em. Another trait of his, like, if he was havin' dinner someplace and he was settin' near a window, he'd just finish his plate and throw it out in the chuck. One time there he went to some peoples' house for Christmas dinner, they weren't from around here and they were quite excited to get the owner of the hotel in to dinner, so Pearly comes, and after they were all done this here lady starts pickin' up the dishes.

"Pearly jumps up. 'Let me do that,' he says. So he loads up every dish on the table in his arms, staggers over to a window — kersplash. The whole works goes into the chuck. 'Now we can take 'er easy,' he says. But this lady, she can't take it easy at all and she says to Pearly, 'That was all the dishes I had.' 'Don't worry about that,' he says. 'We'll get more in the morning.' "

"Oh, he's a terrible man. His wife had no use for him because he was such a terrible guy, he was always shackin' up with one of 'em that liked that kinda life, and once there he was holed up in the Vancouver Hotel just drinkin' and drinkin' — 'course the beer cases had mounted up, dirty clothes and all, so old Pearly, he thought, well it's time somebody cleaned this place up. Somehow he got a tin heater in there, with a couple three lengths of stovepipe and an elbow. He opened the window, stuck the pipe out there, stuck the elbow on, and shovelled these here beer cases and old socks and stuff in. And lit 'er up. Jeez, black smoke was *pourin'* up the side of the Vancouver Hotel, fire engines were roarin', people runnin' around down below, cops come to the door — 'What in sam hill you doin'?' 'Oh, just cleanin' the place up.' "

I wondered if we'd see Pearly around the hotel, but they said he was out sitting his camp. I wondered if he had anything to do with the rigged spar I'd seen on the way to Minstrel.

"Oh no, that's old M'...kayyyy." Hadley spoke it as if he didn't like to have the word in his mouth.

I tried to remember the name of the second oldtimer McAllister told us to look up. "Mackay, is he that old handlogger who works by himself..."

"He works there all by himself but it's not handloggin' — he's got a machine up the hill with a scabline runnin' down to the chuck." A scabline. That was a new one on me.

" — the mainline goes down the hill to a tailhold out in the chuck and the logs slide down hooked onto a runnin' block, like, then he's got the haulback to pull it back. He walks up, sets the choker, starts the donkey, bounces the log around till it gets slidin' down, shuts the donkey off, walks down the hill and unhooks the turn, all by himself — nobody will work with him, you know."

"Mackay," I pondered. "I'm trying to think if that's a guy somebody told me about. What's his first name?" I didn't say I wanted to see him, because I could tell Hadley had a pretty serious gripe against him.

"We just call him Scabby Mackay," Hadley laughed.

"Because he operates a scabline?"

"Well no, he scabbed durin' the strike. It's the only time he could get work, I guess. Ha ha."

THE NEXT DAY WE decided to sneak over and check out this Mackay. I was a bit put off by what Hadley'd said, but I couldn't resist the chance to see a wooden spar in use, although I was also curious to find out why the wood I'd seen at the bottom of the hill looked so old if it was new workings.

When I got there I still couldn't figure it. There was a slight bay with the hill rising steeply behind it. The track up the hill was grown up in alder eight feet high, but there was a line snaking out of the bush to a stiffleg in the water. The dirt around the line looked as if it had been scuffed around recently, but not much. There was a string of grey old logs forming a semicircle with the beach, and floating inside it such a worthless-looking bunch of old broken slabs, skinny saplings and punky-looking chunks I couldn't imagine the purpose for which they had been collected. We tied to a makeshift raft with a couple of stubby pikepoles, a Gilchrist jack and a couple of boomchains on it, with a banged-up skiff tied alongside.

I'd heard a faint hooting noise up the hill, and now I heard it again. I looked up. There was something jostling the bushes a ways up the skidway. I caught glimpses of an aluminum hardhat. In a few minutes a tall, stooped figure was on the beach waving the hat and making an odd hooting noise like an owl. We untied and idled over. The figure was dressed in ragged wool pants with suspenders over a grey Stanfield top. Grizzled would be the word for his overall look. Grizzled from head to heel. And big. Jim Mackay was a lanky, rawboned old logger well over two hundred pounds with no sign of fat. By now, between seventy and eighty years old, he was permanently stooped, but he must have been a good six-four or six-five in his prime. His face was broad with sad big eyes, a much-bent nose, high cheeks and a wide, expressive mouth that had evidently swallowed a few choker knobs in its time. It was a scarred, lined face, tanned, almost mummified by weather, and it looked like trouble.

"Well, well, well, well..." he spoke in a little girlish voice grinning a mysterious grin. He seemed to have been expecting us. Later I found out he'd been watching us come across the channel from up the hill, and started down to meet us.

"I hope we're not interrupting your work," I said.

"Ha! That's a laugh, that is," he hollered. His normal voice was a rapid-fire, aggressive half-shout. I told him we were in the area collecting logging history and were thrilled to find a wooden spar in operation. I wondered if we could go up and take a look. He was amused by this.

"Logging history," he said. "Well you come to the right place. There's more history than there is logging in this goddamn outfit."

"What are you doing here?" I said, nodding toward the collection of broken chunks.

"That's a good question, that is," he said. "Here, put yer bow in here and we'll go have a coffee at my shack."

Normally nothing will stop a logger from getting out logs in the middle of the day but he obviously wasn't as dedicated to production as he could be. I stuck the nose of the skiff into the rocks and he pushed it out carefully to where it would clear the rocks when his weight pushed it down and jumped in. I couldn't get over the feeling he was completely ready for us. He didn't even bother to tell me where his shack was, but of course I knew it was across the other side where I'd seen the orange boat, tucked into a little bay for protection.

Mackay's one-man floatcamp was bigger than it looked from mid-channel, sprawled across a big cedar float. The float logs were sinking, eaten away to a weedy mess of anemones and mussels below the waterline. The parts that were still above the water were weathered grey and speckled with years of caulk boot prints, a thin cap of dry wood with frayed green edges. Here and there some boards were laid down and piled with junk. Oil drums stood about cocked at angles, one covered with a scrap of plywood held down by a rusty shackle. Kinky cable was sticking up everywhere, brittle with rust.

We tied behind his fishboat, a clumsy-looking little troller with a bright orange hull. "That's the *Orange Crate*," he said with a grin.

I went over to look at a cluster of little fruit trees potted in grease pails.

"Now, don't you laugh at my garden," he said. His plan was to establish a floating orchard, but it

Mackay

43

wasn't coming very fast. There were three shacks: a doorless toolshed dipping into the water at an angle, his bunkhouse, shingled and slightly more weatherproof-looking, sitting levelly on skids, and beside it one just like it except new. He'd meant to move into the new one he said, but didn't have time. He went to the middle one and pushed open the door.

"This is the black hole of Calcutta," he announced. The end of one skid stuck out just under the door sill, making a handy step. It was half slivered away by boot caulks. The air inside was heavy with stove oil, the room dirty but not filthy. There were piles of clothes and magazines in every corner, but none that looked more than a few months old. There was nothing rotting. A smoke-blackened Coleman camp stove sat on top of his grease-streaked oil range. A huge fridge stood beside it. It didn't work, but he still kept food in it. An iron cot sagged in one corner, and in the middle of the tiny room a table and a chair with a cushion crushed black and hard. The wall beside the door was festooned with fishing lures, souvenirs of a summer spent trolling in the *Orange Crate*.

"I want to know about Minstrel," I said, when we got seated.

"Ha! Minstrel, eh? You don't have enough time."

"How long have you been around Minstrel?"

"Oh, Jesus, I've been here this last time around—musta bin handloggin' 'n horsin' around here twenty years."

"But you were around here before that?"

"Oh, I was in and out of here. Travellin' back and forth since, oh Christ, I don't know when."

"Were you here for any of these murders?"

"Hah! The only one I know of was when the Indians murdered old Spitz."

"Spitz—was that his name?"

"Yeah, Spitz. Siwash snuffed him comin' down the dock and took his roll. But I never heard tell of any more than that. 'Course there might have been, years ago."

"Merle Hadley mentioned some others, but he couldn't remember details." Mackay's ears perked up at the mention of Hadley's name.

"So you were talkin' to Hadley were ya? I guess he give ya a real earful about what a rotten bastard I was, eh?"

"What's he got against you, anyway?" I was worried about the scabbing business.

"Oh, I'm ostracized around here. They figure I owe 'em money for work they did on my boat, but I ain't payin' it. I don't mind payin' a *thousand dollars* for something as long as I get my money's worth. But when they try to turn around and harpoon me, well bullshit on 'em. Now, to straighten the shaft in that boat—put a bearing in...do a little caulking—NINE HUNDRED AND SOME GODDAMN DOLLARS!" He

roared the words. His voice continually leapt to a roar and fell to a squeak, and twisted and writhed like a cat. He had all the moves of a practiced bullshitter, honed on the floors of the Dominion and Grand and Minstrel Island beer parlours.

"Two years ago last April. Oh, they're mad. They're tellin' everybody about me. Callin' me a scab and everything else."

A skinny cat materialized from under the cot and rubbed against my legs. "See that cat? She's about fifteen years old," he said. "I can't get her fat. Do you know she won't drink milk? Once in a blue moon, that's all." The cat yowled, and Mackay bent down and yowled back, sounding more like the cat than it did itself. Before I could ask another question about his scabbery, he was onto something else. He had taken off his caulk boots. His grey worksocks were stained bright purple. "Look at the dye outta them goddamn shoes!" he said. "It's poisoned me twice already. It's in the leather. Can you bloody well believe we live in a country where it's legal to put out a shoe like that? I've had these things over a year now and look at it!" I remembered the real loggers from my deep past calling caulk boots caulk "shoes" rather than "boots." He was the real Mackay alright.

"WHAT'S THE STORY ON this Pearly?" I asked.

"Do you know where the Dominion Hotel is in Vancouver?" he said. "You look at that sometime and you'll see that's the Sherdal Building."

"You mean there's a connection?"

"His grandfather built that. Pearly inherited it. He was the fair-haired boy."

"What happened? Lose it in a poker game?"

"Hell no, he's still got it. He gits six dollars a day from the estate. He calls that his beer money. Then there's Sherdal and Kimball. Everett Kimball was his stepfather and he had a pretty good camp. Pearly got that too."

"So he's pretty well fixed?"

"Well, he got stuck when he bought that beer parlour. I don't know what he paid for it but I heard ninety thousand. Now Manning offered him forty thousand and he wouldn't take it. But he won't fix nothin. He hasn't put a goddamn cent into it in the fourteen years he's had it. That's why he's got every goddamn nickel he ever made. Tight? When he gets drunk he makes a big sunuvabitch of a noise, you'd think he was a millionaire, the way he talks.

"Oh Jesus, Jean gives 'im shit! Suffering Christ, she locks 'im out of the beer parlour. Drinkin' up the profits. She hit 'im over the head with a case of eggs one time. Laugh! I never laughed so much in my goddamn life." Once Mackay got rolling he just kept on going.

"Jean doesn't drink. Her family came in to work at the big cannery just through the Blowhole down there in Bones Bay. Her father was net man. That's how Pearly run into her. Her brother Dan, he married Irene Dunseith of the Simoom Sound Dunseiths. Her father had the store there, then Dan and Irene had it, and they ran it for years and years and years and years. They sold it just a few months ago, to the guy that owns the pub in Echo Bay.

"Pat Carney give Pearly quite a write-up when she was up here looking for the best logger that time," he said. The Pacific National Exhibition was putting up a trophy for their logger sports competition and wanted to name it after the best logger of all time, so they sent Carney on a search up the coast. This was when she was a columnist on the *Vancouver Sun*.

"For some goddamn reason I'll never understand they ended up picking Panicky Bell, but she come up to Minstrel lookin' for talent and Pearly give her the full load. In her writeup she went on and on about him and his goddamn place. She said, "Every boss logger should have his own beer parlour.""

I asked him who else was in the running for the greatest logger.

"Oh she was askin' about Harold Bronson. Some goddamn liar told her that bullshit about riding the top out of a tree."

Old time loggers couldn't get legendary by shooting it out at the OK Corral, so they pulled stunts. The big names—Johnny-on-the-Spot, Eight-Day Wilson, Step-and-a-Half Phelps, Mickey the Bitch—all tried to outdo each other with outrageous behaviour of one kind or another. Roughhouse Pete had celebrated his last supper at a certain camp by jumping up on the cookhouse table and kicking all the dishes onto the floor. Harold Bronson was supposed to have proven himself the greatest of all the daredevil high riggers by cutting the top out of a spartree and riding it as it fell twenty storeys to the ground.

"You mean he didn't really do that?" I asked.

"I was right there! We were in camp at Central Lake. There was a bear with a cub. They chased it and it got up a sapling behind the camp. Bronson, he's goina climb up and get the goddamn thing. Well, the sapling busts off and they both sorta flop to the ground. So then he bet everybody he could do the same goddamn thing—take his belt and spurs, go up a tree and cut all the limbs off, undercut it and get it ready to go, and hold onto the top as it came down, then jump off the sunuvabitch. I said, 'You're nuts.' 'You put up a hundred dollars and I'll do it,' he said. I said, 'A hundred dollars to see you commit suicide? You're crazy!' That's as far as it went. But this bullshit got around that he *did* it."

Bronson went on to one of the biggest logging jobs on the coast as superintendent at Bloedel's five-hundred-man Franklin River camp, but he didn't last. "He got the fried egg when the amalgamation happened [between H.R. MacMillan and Bloedel in 1951] and after that he was in this camp and that camp and this camp and the other camp—he borrowed a hundred dollars off me there one time."

Bronson was working alone at a floatcamp just around the corner from Minstrel sometime in the sixties when he disappeared. A few days later they found his body floating with a branch hooked through the suspenders. A couple of big seiners had passed through at top speed around the time he disappeared and Mackay thought their wash might have knocked him off the boom. Mackay also opined that being snaky might have had something to do with it.

"When Pat Carney was up here she says to Dunc McIvor, 'How about this Bronson? He's supposed to have stood on the tree as it fell.' He'd just got drowned a little while before. Dunc says, 'Bronson? He couldn't even stand on a boom!' "

Mackay spluttered out the words as if this was the funniest thing he'd said all day. Bronson and him never got along.

I ASKED HIM WHAT IT was about men like Panicky Bell and Roughhouse Pete that made them stand out, when there were thousands of others who worked alongside them, like Mackay himself, that you never heard about. "Well Panicky, the goddamn clown, it was self-advertising. Jesus Christ! You know what he did at Silver Skagit, the goddamn crazy asshole? Y'see, the Americans had the Silver Skagit. And we, as Canucks, did the logging. It was an international project and Panicky was running it.

"Well, they were havin' this dress-up dinner for all the brass, and Panicky came around and invited a bunch of us to come—Roy MacDonald, Herman Smith was there, and Big Bill Byers. A lot of the old bunch, and all of them my size or bigger. Panicky was sittin' at the fifty-dollar end of the table with Knudson and all the goddamn bigshots, and he had us set up at the other end. So then he'd say to these Yanks, 'Hey, you wanta see some real Canadian bush apes? Take a look at those beauties down there at the end.' Dirty bastard!" Like a lot of what Mackay said, this protest had a hollow ring to it—he was more proud than annoyed at being put on display.

"I knew Roughhouse Pete, too, the goddamn prick—excuse my French. Just a real alky. You'd just see him down on Powell Street, by the Union wharf there. He had a big gut on 'im like a laundry bag at the last. Big vee in his pants there. He had a...a...thing on his face about the size of yer finger like a broken blood vessel pumpin' away there. He always had black eyes. Every time he got down on the skid road there he'd get 'em. He was just a booze kitten. He'd sneak a bunch into camp and peddle it. Oh, the lies that the bugger could tell! Just bullshit. The last time him and I were in the same camp was at Reed Bay for McCoy and Wilson. Before he went to the Rock. Then he was at Shenanigan Lake when I was there. I guess he died in the thirties.

"Oh, a rigging tramp like me, I got to know all those bastards. You'd see 'em in camps, you'd see em on Cordova Street, you'd see em on the boat going up. You'd get on the *Cassiar*, get your staterooms and all, and the first place you'd stop would be Lasqueti Island. Well, at every stop you'd go to the rail and everybody'd be there on the dock and there'd always be someone you know. You'd shout bullshit back and forth, and maybe talk jobs. Maybe old Charlie Klein would be there trying to get you to work a couple of weeks for a drum of gas and seven bucks. All the way up it'd be like that, right to Rivers Inlet. It got to be kind of a family affair."

The biggest gathering place of the bush apes was the skid road area of Vancouver's east end, where the hard core types spent their winters in flophouses in the area between Hastings Street and the waterfront, east of Granville Street. The favourite stopping place was the Grand Hotel, whose proprietor, Ernie Clarke, was known as "the logger's friend."

"That was where the whole bunch stayed. At first it was owned by a guy named Tommy Roberts. He was a crook at cards. Evidently he took somebody for a ride. I think this guy came back and bumped him off. The police were all in on it. They made up songs and everthin' else about him. Ennaway, in my time Ernie Clarke had the Grand Hotel and he took care of a lot of guys when they went broke, got 'em jobs and slung 'em down to the boat.

"Sam Graham tells me Ernie Clarke helped a guy get a settlement outa the compensation board one time. It was Pegleg Hoolan, Whitey Hoolan, ooooh he was an awful bastard, he had one leg. I was tendin' hook for him and you talk about a schemin', dirty sunuvagun now, holy Christ. Whitey'd been hit on the head or some goddamn thing, and compo wouldn't go for it. So he sez to Ernie Clarke, if you make sure they don't lock me up I'll put on an act. So he gets some goddamn soap and one thing another, and he grabs the cash register and he wallops on the counter and 'gibbergibbergibber' — he's raving and foaming at the mouth. Ernie phones for the doctor, sez Whitey's taking these spells, you see, from his head injury. That was enough for the compensation and they paid Whitey off. Sam says that was all cut and dried. Whitey had pulled off this goddamn stunt and Ernie Clarke had split with him. But I don't know where in the hell Whitey ever went to after. Disappeared. Nobody ever knows what happened to him."

WE'D STAYED LONGER THAN we'd planned and I'd get up to go but he'd start another story, and I'd be sitting down again. He kept bringing up the fact he was in a hurry to finish up his claim and I was worried about the prime working time he was losing on our account. Finally we got out the door, expecting he would want a ride back to finish the day's work. It was only 3 p.m. "Ah, to hell with 'er. It's too hot to climb that hill now. I'll go over when she cools down. I gotta watch my ticker."

We went back to Hadley's for the night and the next morning went down the Channel for another try at seeing Mackay's wooden spartree in operation. It was around 11 a.m. and his skiff was in the same place he'd left it the day before. I looked over at his shack and saw him just starting over in his big boat. In a few minutes he was beside us.

"I was just comin' when I saw you," he said. He hadn't been at work since we picked him up the day before. We started following his cable up the hill. The logs had gouged a deep ditch in the clay of the hillside, the sides slimy wet and textured with the winding pattern of the mainline. Some places it was two feet deep with mudwater and so steep you had to grab huckleberry bushes with both hands while your feet flew out below. He had a route worked out all the way up and kept shooing us this way and that. He had been up and down so many times, stepping in the same place every time, that there were footholds worn into the clay like an endless boot-pocked stairway.

"See that hemlog right there?" he said between gasps. "That's the one I was tellin' you about I chased them bears up, all three of 'em went up there like a streak of greased loonshit — pardon my Sanskrit — I carry the axe and shovel and bang 'em y'see, to warn 'em off. I wouldn't want to surprise that big old sow."

He showed us another garden, a little patch of roots and rocks about two yards square that he'd dug up and planted with six-year-old seeds, but none of them sprouted. He laughed a laugh that sounded more like a whimper and shook his head in wonder at his own foolishness. The climb made me puff but both Mary and I managed to keep ahead of him. He kept finding excuses to stop and talk about his bears and the song sparrows the crows chased away and show us the edible elderberries. He'd had a heart attack a few years back and he had to watch he didn't overdo it but he still climbed up and down that hill to unhook his logs and wrassle hangups and right now had the hangup of them all, halfway down the hill. "Holy Mexican Jesus, will you look at that mess!" he yowled, waving his dented hard hat at the tangle of logs and stumps and cables.

The tree stood on a bit of a flat with quite a pile of barkless busted chunks pulled up around it in a cold-deck pile. Any working spartree I'd ever seen was bright, with red bark and sticky sap, but this one had been up so long it was grey and weathered. Like the muddy chunks below in his boom, the wood in his cold-deck pile looked worthless to me, but the price of timber was at an all-time high and apparently he got something for them, either as pulp or fuel. It was what they called a salvage claim. The standing timber had been logged eight or ten years before by a Crown Zellerbach contractor, but they left a lot of the small and broken wood and he was cleaning up under a permit from the B.C. Forest Service. But with his heart, his hangups, his bears, his song sparrows, his garden etc., it'd been slow work. He had been forced to go back seven times to beg for extensions to the permit, each time more desperately. The forestry was getting anxious to burn the slash and get the ground back into production, so the ranger swore the current extension was absolutely the last. There were now only two weeks left on it. There were a hundred or so chunks in his pile and he'd only been averaging two down the hill a day. Meanwhile everything was hung up. Mackay got quite sweaty and wild-eyed when he thought about it, so he tried to keep bullshitting and not think about it. He liked to tell us about the days when he was one of the coast's high-production hooktenders, bossing a crew of top-notch loggers and moving out big wood for million-dollar corporations who put their trust in him.

"Bronson was tending hook at Menzies Bay, before the strike of '34. Camp Four, and I was in Camp Three. Tendin' hook. He sez, 'What's that bastard doin' up here tendin' hook? He couldn't tend hook to shovel shit!' This was the kind of crap that he pulled. I called him Bigshot Bronson. Then Jesus Christ, we both landed up at Central Lake." Mackay laughed his crying laugh.

"Me on the goddamn skidder, tendin' hook, and him riggin' on the sunuvabitch. Well, we did have it then, we did have it. Holy Jesus, Jesus Christ, man! He turns around, and he gives me stump riggin'. And when you get to the back end, the goddamn carriage was draggin' on the goddamn ground. The goddamn asshole, he had the block right under the skyline. You could see the blue smoke come off it. And Christ my slack-puller just fouled and everything else and I told the big Finn, who was push, I sez, you better get that rigger up there and I sez and get some goddamn stuff up the tree, I sez, that's what them back spars are made for. I sez I'm not going to set up on that goddamn thing.

" 'Whatza matter McKee, give 'im a chance,' the push sez, 'we're shorthanded.' I sez, 'Shorthanded? Then shut the sunuvabitch down.' And I walked off. I got outta there before the goddamn thing come down. I quit, see."

Many of his stories ended with him walking off the job because the company wasn't doing it right. This was his main theme: the system was too corrupt for a man like him to put up with. That was why he was where he was, poor but honest,

true to the logger's code. I couldn't help thinking of Bob Swanson's poem "The Tame Apes":

> Life to a woodsman is freedom,
> Not measured in dollars sublime
> But to come and go and quit when he please
> Not beg for a job on his bended knees
> Nor toadie to tycoons with rich properties
> Who would see him in hell for a dime.

Mackay could reel off Swanson by the yard. There was a thriving tradition of bunkhouse balladeering in his time, and at different times during our stay he'd just burst out. He recited several ballads by old pals of his, men I'd never heard of before, as well as a couple of his own. I wish I'd copied them down.

I stood under the tree trying to follow his explanation of how he swung his blocks without climbing the tree, using an open-face hook on the passline. After three tries I still couldn't get it. His donkey was an old 10-12 Lawrence, and I was anxious to see it run, but it was out of gas. A little sheepishly he told us he was waiting for his pension cheque to come so he could take a barl down to Minstrel and get some. I thought we were coming up to log, but it turned out he was just showing us around. Until the money came through he was going to spend his time getting his boom in shape. We straggled back down the hill. As we passed the hangup he snatched his hardhat off, slammed it down on the butt of the stuck log, and roared with sudden fury, "Look at that miserable buckskin sunuvabitch—my only good choker down six feet in loonshit, you hoozified cakzicker!" He was so mad he forgot to apologize for his Sanskrit.

I helped him stow a few logs in the pocket and suddenly he was propositioning me to go to work for him. "If I'm not cleaned up by the third of next month I'll lose my deposit," he said. I said we were on holidays, and we had to get home soon to get out our next issue. "How much would you want? C'mon." He kept at it. "I'll take both of you. Browneyes here can cook for us. The two of you for two weeks. Name your price."

Mary glowered at him. She was getting a little tired of standing around watching us, and her eyes were green. After an hour or so I decided to go, saying I had to get back to do some work on my motor. Mackay threw down his pike pole and said, "Ah hell, let's go over and bullshit some more." I threw a glance at Mary, she shrugged, so a few minutes later we were back at his cabin. I noticed a couple of absolutely the most haywire crab traps I had ever seen lying out on the float. They were homemade out of plastic hose and fishnet.

"Are there crabs around here?" I asked. We had a good trap on the *Beaver* and I was thinking how nice it would be to have a feed.

"Oh hell yes, up Cutter Creek. Lots of 'em." He pushed one of the traps with his toe. "You gotta pull these up fast because the crabs can get out." He looked around at his floating junkyard self-consciously. "Everything I got is haywire but I can't fix it because I'm too busy doin' nothing," he said.

Inside, I got him back on the subject of Minstrel.

"You know, old Oscar Soderman was the first guy in Minstrel. He handlogged there before there was anything. It was just him. That must have been before 1900. George Joliffe was in here last fall showing me a book with all this history in it [probably *History of Alert Bay and District*, Alert Bay Museum, 1958.] His family had Harbledown Island. They all lived in a place called Joliffe Bay. Now this book claimed old Oscar came to Minstrel in 1905, but it had to be before that. Because a Finn from Sointula, Ahola, he told me he helped build the first cabins on Minstrel, after Oscar had finished, and I don't think even that was 1905 yet. You can't see it now, but there used to be a building on the beach at Minstrel that old Dick Wong had his cafe in. Now, that building was the first store. I've heard people around here call it the first hotel, but you couldn't a got very many guys in it. It collapsed here a few winters ago. The hotel was built by two guys named Armstrong and Bennett in 1905."

Things were starting to come together a little bit, at least concerning Minstrel's earlier history. I knew the hotel was built sometime in the first five years of the century, when the Knight Inlet area was in the midst of the boom Grainger described in 1908:

> A year ago I came to Port Browning [Port Harvey] and found a district of islands and inlets firmly occupied, in appearance, by man: camps scattered through it; steamers running directly to it; machinery at work; hotels and stores at business — everything old established. An old-timer told me he could remember when the first men came to hand-log... And that dim past was *only seven years ago.*

This period of growth was then cut off by the outbreak of World War I, and the Minstrel Hotel, the bar dry, lay empty until Neil Hood resurrected it shortly following the war's end. He kept it well after Hadley first came in 1925. The man locals remembered only as Izzy the Jew had it during the peak years of the forties. These were the important names connected with Minstrel until Pearly Sherdal bought the hotel in 1960.

Izzy presided over the period of greatest activity. Mackay said sometimes on a Saturday night there, every seat would be taken and guys'd be lined up all around the walls, three hundred at a whack. So many boats jammed together at the dock it looked like mussels on a rock. Nowadays, he said, they didn't even bother heating the building in the winter, and if you wanted a drink you took it in Pearly and Jean's living room. But in busy times every room was packed. In the winter the heat was always bad and the plumbing froze so the guys just pissed out the windows.

"Now, I'm not kiddin' you, you'd take a careful long look before you walked past that place. And stink? Omigod! In the spring, with all those drunks rainin' 'er down all winter, holy snuff-coloured Christ — excuse my Latin — you could smell the place goin' by on the other side of the channel."

Izzy was the opposite of Neil Hood, scrabbling after every penny he saw — literally. The guys would throw pennies in the urinal then watch Izzy come out of the can holding something in his hand and go in the living quarters. They'd signal the whole pub to be quiet, listening for the sound of the water running in the sink, then they'd roar with laughter.

Mackay had a little handlog claim he was working on one time and this fella Billy MacLeod hit him up about going into partners. He'd had Billy pulling rigging different places and he was a hell of a worker but a terrible drinker. He'd drink until he just lost all control. On the plus side he had a harelip and received a disability pension of some kind, not much, but enough to provide him and his friends with a little capital when they needed it most. Right now, he told Mackay, he had three unspent cheques cold-decked at the post office. Mackay took Billy on and they set him up in Room 11 upstairs. Billy wanted to go on a big drunk to celebrate their deal but Mackay didn't, and headed out by himself to string some sticks. When he got back a few days later, Izzy met him at the door all uptight and excited. "You better get up there and do something about that partner of yours," he said. Mackay went up to Room 11 to find Billy'd been erupting from both ends, leaving him encrusted in sturm and drang from head to toe. But one of the distinguishing qualities of the compleat bush ape was a well-developed instinct for ministering to drunk colleagues. Mackay grabbed the cot, rolled Billy onto the floor, booted him awake, and ordered him to get into a tub of hot water while Mackay went down to the store and got him some new clothes. When he was stripped Mackay rolled the soiled clothes in newspaper and told Izzy to burn them. Izzy looked distastefully at the bundle. "Are you sure it's all wrapped?" he said. "Are you sure nothing will come out?..." Mackay yelled at him not to be such a goddamn pantywaist and finally Izzy carried the bundle very gingerly down to the furnace and chucked it in.

When it came time to square up the hotel bill, Billy couldn't find his three pension cheques, which he'd withdrawn from the post office. In his grogginess he was quite heartbroken with the knowledge his favourite drinking pants were at that moment going up in flames, and was sure the cheques were in the left back pocket. Izzy tore down the stairs, flung open the furnace door, and thrust both arms full in to grab the smouldering, bubbling pants, which were giving off thick green-and-orange smoke. Just then Billy returned a little nearer to his right mind and remembered the cheques weren't in the pants anyway, they were inside his pillowcase where he always put valuables when he was expecting to be out of his mind for a lengthy period.

The next day Izzy was serving beer in big bandages, every table asking him how it happened and laughing their heads off.

Mackay liked Billy because even though you could hardly understand what he said, he had a fair wit on him. Mackay valued wit. He thought Panicky Bell was overrated as a logger, but did give him credit for a hell of a sarcastic wit. He wasn't the best in the woods though; that honor Mackay reserved for an old logger named Ed Dahlby, the greatest logging wit of all time. And Billy wasn't bad. Once in the hotel he got a call on the radio phone, so he picked up the mike and said, "McClough here."

There was a pause and the operator said, "I have a call for Mr. MacLeod at Minstrel Island."

"Thih ih McClough at Mineral Island," Billy shouted. He immediately went all red and started slamming his fists when someone couldn't understand him.

"I'm sorry, sir," said this operator very crisply. "You will have to speak more clearly or we won't be able to put your call through the board."

That was too much for Billy.

"Tay your fuhen boar and shove it up your ah!" he roared. The others were all sitting there chuckling at this, and someone said, "Hey Billy, you can't talk like that over the radio."

"Besides, that board of hers is big as a door."

"Oh," Billy said, and turned back to the radio. "I apologize, ma'am," he said. "I thaw ih wah juh a li'l boar."

BILLY MACLEOD WASN'T THE dirtiest man who patronized the Minstrel hotel. That distinction was held unchallenged by an old Finn fisherman whose boat was so greasy even the rats wouldn't stay on it. He dropped in for a binge one time when Izzy had just spent a lot of money fixing up the hotel's plumbing in the hope it would get through the winter without breaking down. Well this old Finn drinks himself stupid and crawls over to the toilet to barf and he barfs out his false teeth. The next morning the urinals are backing out onto the floor and running down the hall. Every drain in the hotel is stopped up. And the old Finn is staggering around asking every-body if they've seen his teeth. He must've taken them out sometime during the night and stashed them somewheres, he figures. Izzy gets someone to tear all his new plumbing apart, and of course at the bottom of the blockage they find the Finn's false teeth. The plumber holds them up with his pliers.

"What do you want me to do with them?"

"Don't bring them near me!" Izzy says, backing away, so the plumber sets them down on the furnace grate. Izzy is wild about what this is costing him, and when the old Finn stumbles back through, Izzy points at the grate and says, "We found your goddamn teeth!"

"Oh, good," the Finn says and stoops down and pops them into his mouth.

"Gee, it sure feels good to have 'em back," he says, grinning all around the room.

"Jumpin' parboiled Christ!" Mackay said, telling us the story. "We was too sick to laugh!"

We spent the next day exploring the pretty little Indian reserve of Matilpi and going up Cutter Creek in a fruitless effort to catch some crabs. We had only three days left before we said we'd be back in Pender Harbour, so we had to head straight south, but we thought we better go have one last goodbye at Mackay. Heading into rock-studded Chatham Channel with the *Beaver*, I realized how much we'd come to feel at home there. When we first came up, I wouldn't take the boat in without stopping to fret over the rash of crosses on the chart, but now I wheeled through with hardly a thought. We had really become a part of this place. I'd absorbed so much of its atmosphere from Hadley, and Mackay especially, I felt like we'd been there for years. I hadn't thought of the magazine in a week.

Mackay was working over at his claim for once, beating on his jackpot with a cracked peavey, and as usual it didn't take much argument to get him to stop for a coffee, this time aboard the *Beaver*. To my dismay, he was still on his kick about having us work for him. I was afraid if he kept at it I would have to say something that would hurt him, and I wanted to part with good feelings. Looking back after all the hundreds of days and weeks I've frittered away since, I can ask myself why I didn't give him a few days, if just for the sake of being able to say we'd helped the last of the oldtime bush apes clean up his last claim. I suppose I thought his little salvage operation was pointless anyway, something he kept up only to have a reason not to join his sisters at their retirement home in Kelowna, and to keep faith with his old lost world of Johnny-on-the-Spot and Step-and-a-Half and Eight-Day and Bronson. I wouldn't have been surprised to find he actually had no sale for the wood at all, and in the end just fed his chunk-boom to the teredos. Also, I hadn't seen him do anything to lessen my general impression that he was no doubt a thoroughgoing old reprobate you'd like less as you got to know more. I met a young fellow later who'd lived around Minstrel, and he had Mackay down as real trouble. "He tried to steal my wife!" the guy said, with such indignation in his voice I could only conclude old Mackay must have made a pretty good stab at it.

Still, I felt I was kind of cheating Mackay, because he'd given me what I'd come looking for. Through him I'd become intimate with Minstrel's glory days, and ever since I've been able to talk about the legendary old names of logging without thinking I might just be making it all up. I never actually knew them, but I knew a guy who did.

OUR LAST CONVERSATION with him was given mostly to his favourite preoccupation—cataloguing the stupidity of the damn fools who ran the show. As far as he was concerned, the country was now so buggered up there was no place left for an independent working man who wanted to put in an honest day's work without kissing anybody's ass. "The scissorbills run everything now," Mackay sighed. "They've about run all the good men off the claim. The timekeepers have taken over."

He looked suspiciously at us. We were obviously in danger of coming down permanently on the scissorbill side of things. "If I lose this claim I don't know what the hell I'll do," he muttered. There was nowhere left for him to go. In the old days, when you got feeling like this, you caught the Cassiar down to Vancouver and hit Cordova Street. But you couldn't go down to the skid road anymore because the fast buck artists had tricked it out as a tourist trap. The last time he'd been down there he couldn't find any of his old watering holes because they all had new names. He got so turned around he ended up putting the hustle on a lady cop. "She probably wouldn't a' bin any good anyway," he said. Then, sensing he'd said something indelicate again, he turned to Mary. "Pardon my French..."

Minstrel was all he had left. He went down in the daytime for grub and freight, but he hadn't been there at night for two years or more. There was no point. There was nobody there but Pearly and his warm beer. I asked him if he thought the place would liven up if they opened the woods up to small operators again.

"Sure they would, but what's the use of talkin' about it? The big cumpnys have all the timber and they aren't ever going to give it up.

"We *know* the big cumpnys run the show. We *know* that. The big cumpnys put us independents out of the way because we show'd 'em up too bad.

What I can't swallow is the way these guys loggin' around here now play along, cuttin' the big cumpny's timber for a percentage. They're not loggers, they're sharecroppers!"

I asked him if he thought there was anything the NDP could do. The B.C. party was in the midst of their brief reign then and the federal party under David Lewis was sharing power with the minority Liberal government. "Oh, that goddamn Lewis, jumping into bed with the Liberals. The goddamn party's shot now, done, buggered. And what for? Just so that goddamn clown can feel important around Ottawa for a few months!" He kept coming back to it, although he said he had no faith in half-assed socialists to begin with.

"What about your boat?" I said. The *Orange Crate* had an A licence for salmon fishing, which was worth its weight in gold at that particular time due to the licence freeze recently brought in by the federal minister of fisheries, Jack Davis. If he couldn't fish it he could sell it for enough to live in comfort for all the years he had left.

"Ah, the goddamn fishing industry is fouled up worse than logging," Mackay shouted. "Davis, that goddamn scissorbill, he's right in with the cumpnys, you know. Jimmy Sinclair, he owns B.C. Packers and Trudeau both. What a goddamn scandal that is. That boat there, I bought it five years ago for twenty-seven hundred. Now I could sell it for twenty-seven thousand. Well, them big cumpnys own hundreds of boats. Thousands. Big, big seiners and packers. Christ, yes. Well, can you think how much that cumpny stock went up on account of this Davis Plan?

"People are so stupid. Us Canadians must be the stupidest people on earth."

WE LEFT HIM STANDING in the door of his black little shack, making a shy little baby-wave and putting on a stagey hurt look. I kept up with Minstrel news when I could after that. The store burned down. Bill Hadley died tragically in an accident at his shop. Pearly's boat was found drifting with no one aboard one day and he was never seen again. People who knew said he did it on purpose because for his type of guy it was all over. The last I heard Mackay was still going, although that was a good while ago. I'm sure he's long dead now. But every time I pick up a newspaper and read about Jack Davis getting re-elected in spite of his fraud conviction, or about Pat Carney signing away Canadian hydro and gas under free trade, I hear old Mackay's cracked voice roaring across the water: "Us Canadians must be the stupidest people on earth."

HOSPITAL LIFE at BELLA BELLA

FLORA C. MOFFAT

BIRTHS AT SEA AND rare diseases, Indian totems, boat parties, and a B.C. coast legend—these were all part of my nineteen-year sojourn with Dr. George Darby at his United Church mission hospital in Bella Bella.

Dense fog enveloped the Bella Bella cannery village on Denny Island as I landed there about 7 a.m. on October 22, 1944 after a long, slow trip up the B.C. coast on the Union Steamship *Catala*. It was during World War II and for safety reasons the steamers did not announce their arrival time, but Oscar Bainbridge, manager of the B.C. Packers plant, met me and assured me that the doctor would soon be along to pick me up. Shivering in the freight shed, I wondered what life was going to be like in this land of islands, boats, and fog. Different from the life I'd known in Ontario, that I felt sure. Finally Dr. Darby arrived in the hospital launch, the *Edward White*, to take me the mile across the channel to the R.W. Large Memorial Hospital in the Indian village on Campbell Island, where I was to take up my duties as nurse.

George Elias Darby had been medical superintendent of the hospital for thirty years before my arrival. Books have been written about his work as medical missionary on British Columbia's central coast, and it is not my intention to repeat what has already been published, but lest anyone think I'm denying him his due I will emphasize at

the outset that he was the mainspring not only of the hospital but of the affairs of the village. As one young Indian boy said, "Dr. Darby's a ten-talent man, and he uses them all." He did indeed.

He arrived in 1912 as an assistant, but the preceding doctor took the next steamer out, leaving Darby as the sole medical aid for a vast area of the north coast. Besides taking charge of the hospital he found he had to wrestle with travel on northwest coast waters in a balky boat, making his way to cases in isolated inlets many miles away, no easy task for the young man from Ontario. But the challenge appealed to him, and when he finished his medical studies, he requested the position of superintendent at Bella Bella hospital. His official tenure began when he returned with his new bride, Edna Matthews, in 1914, and was to last until 1959. He supervised the hospital as it grew from an 8-bed ward to a modern, 28-bed facility. Until 1955 he also ran a Nurses' Training School at Bella Bella. During his 45 years there Darby served the village and the surrounding communities—from Kitamaat, 150 miles north, to Rivers Inlet, 90 miles south—as medical doctor, ordained United Church clergyman, justice of the peace, and jack-of-all-trades, who could repair the church roof or nurse the lighting plant engine back to health. He married the people, buried them, delivered their babies,

Darby's hospital at Rivers Inlet

Dr. George Darby and family at Green's Cannery, about 1940

removed their tonsils, befriended and protected them, and occasionally fined them for drunkenness on Saturday night.

His wife, too, contributed to the community. When Edna Darby arrived in 1914 she held both cooking and sewing classes, and this instruction made a vast difference in the home life of the people. Having both a medical doctor to treat their illnesses and improved sanitation and nutrition in the home, the life expectancy of the people was expanded to such a degree that by the time the doctor retired the population of the village had more than tripled. His own four children, three boys and a girl, were born there.

Soon after my arrival in the village, Chief Moody Humchett decreed that henceforth the white doctor would be known as Chief Wo-Ya-La, the highest. This occasion was the first of many social functions I was to enjoy among the

Indian people, and I am indebted to them for much kindness, both in their homes and on sightseeing trips around the coast in their fishing boats.

BELLA BELLA IS ONE of the most beautiful spots in the world, but there was much to do there besides sightsee. Life in a small hospital can be hectic. From November 1947 until May 1948, Marjorie McDowell, Marjorie Long, and I were the only nurses on staff, although we had first-class help from several Indian girls who acted as nurses' aides. They took care of the housekeeping duties, while Alice Mason did the laundry.

We often had to keep odd hours. I had been there only a short time when I was assigned to night duty. One evening the doctor had been working late at the hospital. As he was leaving he said, "Be sure and get little Beatrice up and dressed ready to go home at 3 a.m." Three in the morning! I was horrified. Beatrice was a young Indian girl who had been at the hospital for more than two years recovering from tuberculosis. When I objected, the good doctor informed me that that was when the steamer would arrive to transport her home to Kitamaat. Such was the way of life in those days, on an island where boats were the only mode of transportation. The islands were twenty miles from the mainland and at the time I arrived there was one boat a week going north and one a week coming back south. Boat day was eagerly looked for—even at 3 a.m.—as it brought the mail, the freight, and a variety of patients and visitors.

The acquisition of a radio telephone in 1947 made life easier. We were able to contact ships and the doctor could consult specialists in Vancouver for the more difficult cases. We could also give advice to the sick and injured en route to the hospital, especially when long distances had to be covered before patients reached us. Many patients arrived after travelling many miles in fishboats, in all kinds of weather. One young woman suffered a severe hemorrhage after giving birth to twins at her home in Kitamaat. She travelled the long distance to Bella Bella, 150 miles, in her husband's boat, with an Indian friend in attendance. Thanks to the radio telephone we had news of her condition and everything was ready for immediate action at the hospital when she arrived. With the help of several blood transfusions she made a fine recovery, but it might have been a different story had the hospital staff not been prepared.

The new antibiotics—penicillin and streptomycin—did even more to revolutionize our working lives. The TB patients responded well to streptomycin therapy—some of the results were almost miraculous.

1948 was the start of a new era. The provincial government took over financial responsibility for the hospital, which until then had been assumed

Totems on Wannock River near Owikeno Lake

by the Board of Home Missions of the United Church of Canada. At last we were able to hire our full quota of nurses.

The hospital was always in need of new equipment, although many families would donate gifts of furniture and money as memorials, and this did much to keep the hospital furnishings up to date. Dr. Darby encouraged them to do this rather than spend a lot of money on tombstones. Many church groups throughout the province and the country sent gifts of money, linen, toys, and books, as well.

Still, we had to "make do" a lot of the time. During a long cold snap one winter, the lake that was our water supply went dry and we were without water for six weeks. This really taxed our ingenuity, but we managed. The village of Namu loaned us a large clean tank—usually used for soaking fish nets—and this was placed in the hospital basement. Every morning Namu sent another tank filled with fresh water, and the men on staff pumped its contents into the tank in the basement of the hospital. It was such a relief when spring came and brought an adequate supply of water to the hospital taps again, and we no longer had to pack water in buckets.

Whatever the condition of our equipment, however, there were always people coming to the hospital for treatment. Some patients stand out as special in the life of every hospital, and little Nellie was certainly one of them. She came from Takush, an Indian village ninety miles to the south. Though she was a year old, she looked more like a baby of three months; she was so sick and weak from undernourishment that she was unable to sit up, and did not even have the strength to utter more than feeble whimpers. She was also suffering from a severe skin condition. Recovery came slowly. It took weeks and weeks of careful nursing before she finally began to im-

prove, gained steadily, and became the darling of the place. It was a sad day for the staff when she left for home, but it was satisfying to compare her healthy, smiling face to our memories of the pitiful infant of a few months before.

I remarked to Dr. Darby once that one of the patients had an unusual disease. "If you stay here long enough, Flora," he replied, "you'll see everything." He was right.

Vincent was first admitted to hospital when he was a baby. He was born with fragile bones, and suffered more than fifty fractures by the time he was twelve years old. Usually this condition is outgrown by the time the victim reaches puberty, but although Vincent stopped having fractures, his bones were never strong enough to bear his weight so he had to spend his life in a wheelchair. He became so used coming to the hospital to have various broken limbs mended that when Dr. Darby was away he was able to tell the relieving doctor where he would find the proper splints for his arm.

Another little fellow had Toni Franconi Syndrome. This is a disease in which the patient does not have adequate growth hormones and seldom lives past the age of six or seven years. The boy I saw was, at six, the size and weight of a three-year-old, though he had normal mental development. He died before he reached seven. There are few instances of this syndrome on record in Canada.

Something else I had not seen before was Van Recklingham's disease; the patient had hundreds of small cysts growing on his skin. These three diseases are rare in any locale, so I certainly didn't expect to encounter all three of them in a remote area on the north coast of British Columbia, but there they were.

We also treated many burn cases. Mary Anne, aged two, was badly burned when her clothing

Rivers Inlet Hospital

occasion to dispute that statement more than once. One January I was going to Vancouver for a short holiday. Matthew, a six-week-old Indian baby born with club feet, came with me to have his feet corrected. We boarded the steamer around 5 p.m. and the ocean was as calm as a mill pond. At 8 p.m. a stewardess came to my cabin to say we were running into a severe storm and asked me to make sure the baby was securely tucked in. In a matter of minutes the storm broke. We thrashed around Queen Charlotte Sound for eleven hours in a ninety-mile-an-hour gale. It was my first and only experience of seasickness and I took a dim view of the whole episode. Sadly, although Matthew survived the storm, he never returned to his home. While he was in Vancouver he got pneumonia and died.

WHEN I WENT TO Bella Bella in 1944 the hospital operated a fishermen's hospital every summer in Rivers Inlet, then one of the finest areas for sockeye salmon in the world. Several staff members from Bella Bella went to the inlet hospital each year. I spent six summers there, and enjoyed every minute of them. One medical student from Toronto was impressed with the beauty of the inlet and commented that he knew lots of people in Toronto who would pay good money for the trips he had taken that summer. "To think I get paid for doing what I do," he marveled.

Most afternoons the doctor, a nurse, and usually a medical student made trips to various camps where we held clinics and looked after the sick and injured. It was also a good opportunity to round up the children and give them their immunization shots. Although it was supposed to be a fisherman's hospital, one summer we delivered five babies in five nights to fishermen's wives. Naturally we didn't have any nursery facilities, and finding places to store all these little newborns was quite a challenge.

The medical students had some varied and unusual situations to cope with at Rivers Inlet. Clarence Cohoe accompanied a pregnant woman who was travelling to the hospital aboard the *Laurel Point III* in 1949. The mother-to-be was settled on the deck under a tarpaulin tent by the mast, and Clarence crawled in to check her condition from time to time. For the rest of the journey he stood by the skipper, Ling Choy, who told him that the previous year a baby had arrived right on board, just as they passed Millbrook Cove. He wasn't anxious for a repeat performance, but Clarence assured him that they had plenty of time. The trip from Margaret Bay to Rivers Inlet involved a short stretch of open ocean, past Tie Island Cap to Cranston Point, which shook up boat and patient in the Pacific swells, but it wasn't until the home stretch, inside Rivers Inlet, past the "Haystack" and the Skoo-

was ignited by her young brother who was playing with matches. She was treated and, when the wounds were ready, they were covered with skin grafts. Another burn victim walked into the hospital one morning at 6 a.m. wearing only a blanket. His boat had caught fire and sunk, and although he had escaped alive, he had second- and third-degree burns over most of his body. He remained with us while he received first-aid treatment and recovered from the initial shock, but by this time plane service was available on the coast, so we had him flown to Vancouver where he could not only receive more extensive treatment but would be closer to his family.

I was often amazed at the stoicism of the people living in remote areas. I remember a fisherman arriving at Rivers Inlet hospital with an abscess on his shin. It was huge and painful, and Dr. Darby suggested he would have to lay up for a week or ten days. It was the middle of sockeye season, and it meant losing valuable fishing time, but the doctor assured him it was the only way his leg would heal properly. He had the abscess drained under general anaesthetic, but the moment he was fully awake he donned his clothes and went back to work. He did turn up for daily dressings for several days, and only lost a few hours' work.

Once we had a food poisoning incident. Three sisters became ill from eating salmon eggs, and one of them died. The remainder of the food was sent to the provincial laboratories and Dr. Dolman, the director, found a botulism which had been responsible for serious illnesses in other parts of the province and in many other countries. For the first time he had the opportunity to take accurate figures on the degree of toxicity, and to determine what amounted to a lethal dose. From this knowledge an antitoxin was developed, which is now kept in hospital refrigerators in all places where the problem is apt to occur.

But accidents and illness were not the only dangers we faced on the northern coast. When I left Ontario one of my friends remarked, "It's a good thing the Pacific Ocean is so calm." I had kumchuck, that labour started in earnest and the baby arrived before the boat could reach the hospital.

Over the years the old hospital on Rivers Inlet became more and more decrepit. With the advent of planes and faster boats it was closed in 1957, replaced by a first aid station at Wadhams Camp with a medical student in charge for the summer. Patients needing hospital care were transported to Bella Bella.

There was still no nurse or doctor at the Indian villages of Klemtu and Kitamaat, and these places were not receiving much in the way of medical attention. The Bella Bella doctor wasn't free to leave the hospital for several days at a time, so one year I was elected to go on the Indian agent's boat to visit these places. I was away nine days and had a busy time, especially at Kitamaat where there was a bad flu epidemic. I treated more than forty people with penicillin and mild sedatives. One young girl had a severe ear infection following a mastoid operation. I had her taken to the hospital, but the infection had been too severe and longstanding, and she died shortly afterwards.

There were five lighthouses reaching from Klemtu to Smith's Inlet, most of them in isolated places, and the doctor made it his business to see that the people living there were looked after, too. He now had a radio phone on the hospital boat, and all the lighthouses were equipped with one, so he could phone to say he was in the neighbourhood and inquire if they needed any medical care. One time this paid off. Dr. Darby and Reverend Johnson had gone to Rivers Inlet in the late autumn to conduct a funeral. On their return trip to Bella Bella they decided to call at Addenbroke lighthouse, at the entrance to Rivers Inlet. When they landed, the lighthouse keeper greeted them with the words, "Am I glad to see you." His wife had just delivered her baby two months prematurely and he needed help.

At this same lighthouse, Dr. Darby once took the lightkeeper's wife home following surgery on her knee. She was in no shape to clamber up the rocks, but it was a calm day and the hospital launch was able to pull in close to shore. The lady was lifted on a stretcher by the derrick used to land freight. It was a bit hair-raising for the patient, but it was the easiest solution to a tricky problem.

FROM 1914 TO 1952 Dr. Darby carried the burden of the medical work alone except in the busy summer months, when there was extra staff to look after the work at Bella Bella and to take care of the Rivers Inlet hospital. As well, a qualified doctor would take over at Bella Bella while Dr. Darby went to the fishing grounds. This doctor would remain after the summer rush ended, so the Darbys could take their holidays.

The volume of work was steadily increasing, and in 1952 Dr. Ruth Alison, a recent graduate from Toronto, arrived as the first full-time medical assistant. Ruth was warmly received and endeared herself to everyone; she also did a splendid job. After Ruth left, Dr. Darby always had full-time assistance with the work at Bella Bella.

When the Darbys retired, a farewell party was held at Wadhams Camp on Rivers Inlet, at the height of the fishing season, when there would be in the neighbourhood of a thousand boats fishing on the Inlet. Three thousand people gathered for the occasion, a company composed of members from many nations and from many walks of life. There were Japanese and Chinese, Scots and Irish, Swedes and Norwegians, whites and Indians. There were government officials, churchmen, company managers, fishermen, and loggers, the educated and the illiterate, the rich and the poor, and somehow we were all brothers and sisters who had come to declare our love and devotion to this humble man and his wife for the services they had rendered over the years. Most of us had personal cause to be grateful, for I'm sure during his tenure he had ministered to us all in some way.

I think the Reverend Dr. Peter Kelly, a Haida Indian from the Queen Charlotte Islands, paid a fitting tribute at a church service held in Dr. Darby's honour. He used as his text these words from Paul's letter to Titus: "This is why I left you at Crete; that you might amend what was defective." Dr. Darby tried, successfully, to amend the physical, social, and moral problems over the years, and he continued working as coordinator of United Church hospitals until his death in September 1962.

The R.W. Large Memorial Hospital has carried on Darby's work. In 1987, the 85th anniversary of its founding, the hospital is a 23-bed institution with a staff of 35, continuing to serve a large area of the north coast. David Preston, Ian Chisholm, Roger Page, Robert Henderson, Pat Arnup, Ray McIlwain, Sandy Campbell, Stuart Iglesias, Duncan Etches, and Mark Young have made valuable contributions to the work of the hospital as medical superintendents since Darby's retirement.

I HOPE I HAVE not given the impression that all things were sweetness and light. We had our share of tragedy and dark days. However, making needlepoint tapestry has been a hobby of mine for many years, and I soon discovered the dark threads were as needful as the bright ones. Without the dark threads, the bright ones are a meaningless blob of colour. So it is with the tapestry of life. The dark days make the good ones more exciting and meaningful.

84 YEARS
in BELLA COOLA

A Conversation With George Draney

BARRY BROWER

IN 1885, AN adventuresome young man arrived by train in Westminster, British Columbia. This was the western terminus of the recently completed transcontinental railroad, and the enterprising twenty-year-old, Tom Draney, had worked his way west from Ontario by helping to build it. He had come to the coast on the advice of his cousin, Robert Draney, who had preceded him by about ten years and was now the successful owner of two fish canneries in the central coast area of the province.

Both Draneys were known as hard workers. Their families had emigrated to Ontario from county Armagh in Ireland to escape the potato famine of the late 1840s, and Tom Draney was looking for an opportunity. He was at first not too enthusiastic about remaining on the west coast—he didn't much like the damp, rainy climate—but cousin Bob encouraged him to stay on and offered him a job establishing a new cannery on a rocky chunk of shoreline at Namu. The young man accepted, and subsequently

George Draney

moved on to the Nass and Skeena areas of British Columbia's north coast, where he worked for several years as a cannery manager.

But working for someone else has never been part of the Draney fabric, and Tom was no exception. He wanted to run his own cannery and began to search about for another opportunity. Then someone told him about a lush and verdant valley at the head of Burke Channel in the central coast region. This "pretty little place" in the mountains was called Bella Coola and described as a suitable location for a new cannery. Friends encouraged him to get a grub stake together for the winter and try his luck in the predominantly Indian community. In 1892, two years before the influx of a large group of Norwegian settlers from Minnesota, Tom Draney staked his future in the remote mountain community.

In many ways, things went well for young Draney. He purchased an eighty-acre tract of land for three hundred dollars (it is still in the family), and he met and married Olea Marie Fosback, the daughter of one of the Norwegian settlers. On January 15, 1903, the first of eleven children, George Herbert, was born to the couple.

During this period there had been some problems in getting a cannery started, for Tom Draney was long on experience but short in funds. Then he met John Clayton, the owner of the local Hudson's Bay store, and, in what appears to have been a snap decision, the two agreed to enter into a partnership. Clayton provided what had heretofore been missing: the financial capital to get the cannery started.

George Draney, now into his ninth decade and looking twenty years younger, tells of the simple agreement the two men signed.

They were in Victoria and dad said, "Well, I don't know any lawyers, but let's go up the street here and the first one we come to we'll go in. How about that?" Clayton agreed, and that's how it happened. And so, in 1900 or 1901 they got the cannery started.

First off my dad would make a deal with some wholesale house for, say, five thousand cases of Sockeye. That's the only salmon they canned in those days. He'd go to wherever you bought steel and get enough tin plate for five thousand cases. The tin plate would come in large sheets like plywood and then be cut into smaller sections. They would roll these sections into the shape of a can, solder in a bottom, pack in the fish, and then solder on a top. The entire can was soldered by hand and they were perfect cans.

Chinamen did all the work. There wasn't a cannery on the coast that didn't have Chinamen. They were the next thing to a machine. They were good.

They cooked the fish after putting them in big trays. You'd stack them up and wheel them into a

Retort [basically, a very large pressure cooker]. The Indian women would pack the fish and the cans would have a small hole in the top to allow steam to escape. After cooking, the cans would be sealed with a drop of solder. As they cooled it was almost like a rifle range in there because you could hear those cans go "poonk." If the can seals right it pulls the top down, you see. When they were cool enough to handle the Chinese would use a little tool like a tuning fork and they had a couple of those, one in each hand, and they'd go over those cans. It sounded like a little tiny machine gun going, a kind of "thrrr, rat-a-tat-tat," testing those cans for sound. There was no mistaking because if there was a dull, thuddy plunk, a dead sound, then the can wasn't properly sealed. And they hardly missed this rhythm and the bad can would be laying out on the floor. It was picked out like lightning.

Dad stuck with it about three or four years until he couldn't stand the smell of fish anymore. It just got to him I think—I never saw him open another can of fish in his life.

THE REMOTE GEOGRAPHICAL location of the Bella Coola valley has always presented problems for those interested in large-scale economic development. Situated at the head of a deep channel suitable for ocean-going ships, Bella Coola has nevertheless been by-passed as a west coast port because it is too far from the main shipping channels—nearly 60 miles—to make it economically worthwhile. At the same time it is three hundred miles eastward by the only road to the nearest trading center. And though it is a mere two hundred or so air miles to Vancouver, it is over six hundred by the road. The road itself is relatively new—it was completed in 1954 and remains predominantly unpaved to this day. Access to Bella Coola has never been easy, and George has some interesting comments to make about the MacKenzie or "Grease" Trail, long believed to be an Indian trading route through the mountains.

I guess at first the Hudson Bay Company had its supplies come in by steamer, the "Beaver" I think it was called. It came from Victoria and not Vancouver because until the railroad came through, Vancouver was nothing. Just a bunch of beachcombers there. It was a weekly service.

Any travel by the white man to the Interior was done by pack horse up the telegraph trail to Precipice. It was a much easier and faster grade [than the MacKenzie trail]. And, too, what I think common sense will tell you, if there was any trading to be done by the Indians in eulachon grease, which was in containers weighing maybe a hundred pounds or so, you wouldn't pick the highest mountains to go over such as you have with the grease trail. MacKenzie didn't mention

57

anything about a trading trail over the mountains. As a matter of fact there was no trail. He came across the mountains using a compass.

It [the Grease trail] may have been a hunting trail perhaps, but there was no one living up in that high country. The villages were located any place there was an abundance of fish—in the valley as far up as Stuie and on the plateau at Anahim Lake and Fish Trap [Nimpo Lake]. It wouldn't make sense to pack those heavy containers over six thousand foot mountains when it was easier and closer to go by Precipice. And the Indians out at Kimsquit [mouth of the Dean River] could take their war canoes up the Dean River. It is tough going but they could get up there. They used to go through that canyon at low water. It's only a short distance anyway so once they got inside it they were o.k. And they'd meet other interior Indians at Tanya Lake or Salmon House.

Salmon House was a place where the salmon couldn't get any farther because of a falls on the Dean and all the Indians had to do was go down there and spear them. They had smokehouses and there were lots of berries so the Indian women could be out picking berries while the men fished and dried the catch. The Indians wouldn't take the fat salmon like we do. They wanted them half spawned-out because if there was too much fat they'd go rancid. They dried the fish for winter and I've seen them stacked up like cordwood in the old Indian buildings down here. This is where the eulachon grease came in. They would dip this dried fish into the eulachon grease and that way they get the fat, you see. The way the eulachon grease is done now is different. They used to rot the fish rather than boil it to get the oil out. I don't think the modern Indians would eat the stuff the oldtimers ate—it stunk to high heaven. But I thought it was good.

The Indians also used to go up and down the river trapping beaver, otter, mink, and so on. They were terrific canoeists but the young Indians today don't know anything more about a canoe than I do. They used something like a little adze with a blade like a chisel, beveled one way, and they would hack away at a cedar log. If they wanted more beam to the canoe they would put boiling water and hot stones on the inside to stretch it out. At the end they would start a controlled fire on the inside to smooth and polish it. Some of these canoes were upwards of sixty feet long, with high bows and sometimes sails, and I would say they could average about six or seven miles an hour paddling. I'm told they could go about twelve, chasing somebody or fighting. They could probably make a hundred miles in a day.

When Norwegian settlers arrived in Bella Coola they would freight stuff up the river by canoe. It was a lot easier than backpacking it and there weren't many horses then. They had pretty much

the same way of living in Norway you know, and that's why they fitted in here like a glove. They dried their fish, had their garden plots, made their own cheese—that's what they had to do to live. Both groups were faced with the same problems in the valley and the Norwegian ancestors had probably lived in Norway much the same as the Indian. The Indians caught on to the white man's ways pretty fast, too, because it was an easier way to live.

DESPITE WHAT APPEAR to be rather obvious geographical limitations to commercial development in the Bella Coola valley, the early white settlers were hopeful, even convinced, that it was only a matter of time until it happened. Today, their grandchildren are still waiting. At the turn of the century, progress seemed inevitable and there was considerable speculation that a proposed west coast terminus of the northern railroad would be located at Bella Coola. It was not to happen. A more logical route to Prince Rupert was chosen instead. Many Bella Coola residents altered their lifestyle drastically during this period, with an eye to cashing in on their investment when development finally came. One of these individuals was Tom Draney, who saw agricultural possibilities for his land and began clearing the large cedars and cottonwood, little realizing that he was laying the groundwork for a career of logging—nearly sixty years in length—for son George. The elder Draney worked the land until his death in 1927, but George's early experience clearing trees from the property had given him a taste for the logging business.

We logged the timber off our property with horses, put it in the river, and tried to drive it down to the salt water, but we lost about half the timber. There was a Bella Coola logging company then [in the 1920s] and the idea was to put a booming ground in at the mouth of the river and charge a fee for this service. I kept working breaking up log jams in the river with a peavey and wading up to my waist in ice water all day. There were lots of channels for the logs to hang-up in, but we hoped they would get down to the beach pretty much on their own. It wasn't too successful, but after that I started taking contracts on chunks of timber all over the central coast. There must have been seventy-five or a hundred of us independent operators contracted to Pacific Mills [later Crown Zellerbach] in Ocean Falls.

There were three fairly large [independent] outfits on the Queen Charlotte Islands. Allison's was one, a fella by the name of Kelley, and an old fella by the name of Morgan. They supplied half the wood Pacific Mills used. The rest of us provided the rest. Pacific didn't do any of its own logging at the time. You had to sell your logs to the pulpmill in Ocean Falls because of the problems of getting the logs across Queen Charlotte Sound. And there was no way Pacific wanted anyone else to ship to Vancouver. There was no way to do it if you were a small operator. There was just too much risk.

Pacific had a monopoly. The government was getting panicky in the late 1800s because people were settling up the coast and were having a tough time making it, so I guess Pacific Mills said they would start a pulp mill up the coast if the government would give them a bunch of timber. So of course the government bent over backwards and gave them the whole bloody country! As far back as I can remember the map was covered with their land holdings. And what the company did was to take the front part of a valley that had lots of timber in it and block everybody else. They were paying so much an acre, just a few cents, to hold it. They figured they could hold a whole valley by just having the first mile of it; they could stop anybody else from getting in. The really good areas, they took pulp leases on those and they would take a big enough block so they would make sure nobody else got in there. I think they were paying fifty cents a thousand board feet, and less, on some of those pulp leases. Some of those contracts are still in effect.

The only people who could do anything about it were those companies on the Charlottes. They finally got fed up with the situation in Ocean Falls and built Davis rafts [a raft made out of tiers of logs bound by cable] which would stand the sea.

What they were trying to do was get their logs to market. Even here in the Bella Coola valley the company had large holdings and the settlers would want to sell them timber and only be offered fifty cents a thousand for it. We knew that down below it was worth a hell of a lot more than that. But Pacific didn't need it and that's all they would offer. When someone complained they just said, "Keep the goddamn stuff and pay taxes on it then." So they got practically all the settlers' timber for nothing. And anyone who logged for

them got their contract limited because the company didn't want you to make too much because you might start getting ideas, see. What you did get was barely a livable wage.

Andy Gibbs and Chuck Smith moved into the valley and we formed an informal alliance. Meanwhile, someone had invented the "Oregon Dog" [a flat boom of log cabled together with spike-like objects, the dog, driven into the logs to hold them in place] and you could get across the sound with it. The three of us shipped our timber together and that little invention saved us. Later the barges started coming in to get our wood.

There wasn't enough government timber to go around and so if there was government timber in an area where Pacific was working they wouldn't let us use their roads. Or if new government timber was put up Pacific would outbid us. Or if you had, say, spruce to sell to the mill, they would say, "No, we want cedar." Oh, it was a real monopoly. At one point they told Andy that if he put up any more timber in one particular area, they would break him, so Andy had to quit. Chuck and I continued on for a while. We got some timber from the settlers and I got some from Macmillan-Bloedel. Still, I would offer something for timber and Pacific would go and up the offer a bit and you knew it was like batting your head against a stone wall. But I did have a little bit of a quota and that kept me going.

The trouble now is that the unions have got in and they don't like us gyppo loggers because we're willing to work hard and do a lot of things and the union says, "Hell, don't do that." They want so many hours a day and the gyppo can't live that way. If you've got a storm out there and it's Saturday night are you gonna wait until Monday to go down and see if there are any logs left? It's as simple as that. In the old days we kept things small and did them ourselves. There's still good men, but if you hire too many people who don't take the interest you do, who want to watch the clock, then you're gonna fall down.

Davis raft

Pacific Pulp Mill at Ocean Falls

I started out with a cross-cut saw and spring-board and had to be a jack-of-all trades. But when machines came along you started specializing more. It used to be that five or six men in a camp could do everything but now you ask somebody to do something and they say, "No, that's not my job, go get someone else." An engineer used to be responsible for his machine—his reputation depended on it. Today, it breaks down and he says, "So what?"

It's a lot easier now. Nobody wants to work more than they have to. But why don't we put on the brakes a little instead of demanding more and more all the time, making it easier. Doing less work. And demanding more consumer goods. Today if there's something needs to be done and you can't do it, you let it go because you can't afford to have it done by someone else. In some ways you're not as efficient as you were before. We have a tendency now to buy a fifty thousand dollar machine to do a ten thousand dollar job because it's easier.

A T EIGHTY-FOUR years of age George Draney is in impressive physical and mental shape. He has a clear and amazingly wrinkle-free complexion for a man his age; strong, sharp facial features, rosy cheeks, and a shock of only partially thinning gray hair. He retains a great deal of physical mobility, and though he has been slowed somewhat by arthritis lately, you can still see him driving tractor and helping to work by hand the property that has been in his family all these years. Two daughters still live in the valley. There have been setbacks: his wife died in the early seventies and his only son was killed in a boating mishap in 1975, but George retains a positive outlook on life and is proud of his accomplishments. He has a strong but relaxed personality and has made a success of his life in traditional ways, through hard work and opportunism. Politically, his views reflect these conservative ideals, and though he might be criticized for applying these values too casually as a solution to complex modern problems, the fact remains that this approach has worked for him and he is a contented, healthy, and materially comfortable person as a result.

I try and keep active, and I've always had lots of exercise and been out in the open. I eat anything, but not a lot of it. I come from a long-lived family. Another thing, I guess I've always been interested in what I'm doing. I'm curious and I want to see how other people do things. Even today, I go out and see how other people are logging and so on. If I lost interest in all these things I don't know what I'd do with myself. I'd just sit here and grow old, I guess.

60

Harry Osselton poses in the mouth of a Finback whale, Naden Harbour, 1935

WHALING STATIONS
of the
QUEEN CHARLOTTES

WILLIAM HAGELUND

A T EITHER END OF the Queen Charlotte Islands are the decaying remains of two of B.C.'s most successful whaling stations. Naden Harbour on Graham Island, and Rose Harbour on Kunghit Island processed hundreds of whales a season from 1910 to 1941. Canadian members of Captain Ahab's tribe set out from these stations in search of the elusive vapour blow that signalled a whale, and they harvested the herds of Blue, Finback, Sperm, and Humpback whales off the West Coast.

There were other whaling stations in B.C., all on Vancouver Island—Kyuquot, Sechart, and Page's Lagoon before World War II, and Coal Harbour after. Sechart was the first, and Kyuquot recorded the most whales caught, but the Queen Charlotte stations are known and remembered for their isolation, their thirty-odd years of service, and their violent storms.

Rose Harbour, situated on the south side of the

rock-strewn Houston Stewart Channel, had access to the Pacific via Rose Inlet. This put it less than an hour's travel from the whaling grounds—an advantage over placid, sheltered Naden Harbour that cost dearly in adverse weather. The entire area is a sailor's nightmare, offering unexpected, conditional shelter to the knowing, and anxious, if not disastrous, moments to the ignorant. Captain Dode MacPherson, a whaler from 1916 to 1919, had vivid memories of Rose Harbour. "If the weather was good, we might lay off and let the boat drift during the night, but we seamen still stood our watch while everyone else could grab some shut-eye. Even the fireman could bank up his fires and bunk down for a few hours. The weather up there was atrocious, perhaps I should say abominable, unpredictable, and always adverse, and the currents contrary. But that's where the whales were, so that was where we went! We had a lot of fog up there, and when it wasn't

Charlie Watson standing on the belly of a large Blue whale, en route to Rose Harbour, 1924

foggy, the wind would be blowing. Often I swore it blew continually, and only paused to shift around and blow again from a different direction. The damnable thing about Rose was, there wasn't a decent place to anchor and get away from the weather. Even Sperm Bay didn't have good holding ground, unless you went right up to the head end and snuggled in behind the island.

"Those damn Willies would spring up in the middle of the night and shake you loose. Then we'd have to heave up the anchor, stow the chain, and steam around in the pitch blackness to find a place out of the wind in which to try again. Anthony Island, off the west coast, had good holding ground, but it was only a lee for a southerly wind; if she backed up to the west, we had to get the hell out of there, too. I didn't like Rose too much. We only went in there when we had whales, or needed grub or coal.

"The weather was better up at Naden, more steady, and we could spend more time whaling, and there were several good anchorages when we couldn't."

Charlie Watson had an eye for the rugged beauty of the Charlottes when he was an engineer on the whalers in the 1920s and 1950s. He talked at length about the natural sanctuary for the creatures of the wild, and the many artifacts of the aboriginal history of the area.

"We put in at Anthony Island in 1956, and I had a chance to go ashore and look around. I was sort of pointing out the sights to the other guys, but my god, I was shocked to find hardly anything left of the old graveyard. The only totem poles or lodge poles left were those rotting on the ground. There was nothing standing! Why, when I was there last with Willis Balcom, in 1923, there were dozens of totem poles, and more canoes than I cared to count. Know how they buried their chiefs? In a canoe, placed high up on posts so the animals can't get them, and their families were laid out in boxes around the base of the clan totem pole. God, they were big. All carved with the legendary symbols that told the family's story. They were very forboding to see, all leaning at various angles, glaring down at you as you entered the woods where they were hidden. The Indians wouldn't set foot on the island; they claimed it was haunted. But someone, probably tourists or fishermen, tore down all those totem poles and carted them away. How they did it, I can't guess. They were tremendous things. But there wasn't even a bleached bone left!

"Yes, it's all coming back to me as we talk. There was another graveyard by an old Indian village down near the south end of Kunghit Island, but we never put in long enough to go ashore. But many of those old places have since been renamed in honour of the old whalers, like Balcom Inlet, Larsen Point, Orion Point, Germania Rock, and Grant Bank. Heater Harbour was named after Bill Heater, and Garcin Rocks after Alfus. There's a few more, but I can't put my finger on them right now.

"It's a great place, if you don't mind being a bit remote. You know, I believe it would be impossible for anyone to die of starvation in the Charlottes during the summer months. There were always deer close at hand at the head of those bays, and around Rose there was a special breed of elk that had been imported to the islands years before. They were very good eating, if you were lucky enough to shoot one," he chortled, recalling a happy incident of the past. "For anyone with the minimum of resources and ability, there was all kinds of berries, fish, fowl, and game available. But during the winter months it could be a pretty lonely and hungry place if you got into trouble. I believe the only hospital even now is at Charlotte City, and for a long time the only road there ran from the City up to Port Clements' beer parlour."

Charlie recounted a story involving Fisheye Thompson, another whaling engineer, to illustrate the plight of whalers drying out in such lonely outposts as Kyuquot, Rose, and Naden Harbours in the days before air travel and nearby beer parlours.

"Fisheye was a bit of an unstable chap at the best of times—a top-notch engineer, yes sir. Indeed he was. He was a man who could keep any bucket of bolts steaming right along, but he

62

Rose Harbour Station

required a drink or two to do it and still keep his peace with the world. He had a notorious short fuse whenever his drinking supply ran out, and during one of those occasions, Buster Brown's fireman earned a crack across the head with a wheel spanner, that sent the poor man to hospital. Just because he had knocked a cock open on a tank full of lubricating oil, and it all drained down into the bilge!

"Hell, you know how it was around those places. If a man wanted a drink bad enough, there was always someone who would sell it to him, for a price. Why, even Bill Heater on the *Grant* found his standard compass drained of the alcohol, and water substituted. I'll bet someone paid a good price for that poison. Yes, there was always a little squeeze to be found around Rose Harbour when I worked out of there. I guess the term 'squeeze' came from the fact that anyone daring enough to risk his job to bring booze into the station could squeeze the last penny out of those dried-up drunks that needed it so badly! God knows, after a month or two of sobriety, those guys would have sold their own mothers for a drink. Of course it was almost worth your job to have it in your possession. The company was death on it. They'd had a lot of trouble from drinking during and after the war.

"Well, poor old Fisheye was desperate. His supply had run out, and no one at Rose had any they would sell him. So, when the *Gray* came in, Fisheye went after the strange little steward they had aboard her in those days, and managed to buy a few bottles of suspicious-looking stuff. God knows where that steward got it, but it must have been nearly poison. Well, Fisheye knocked back a couple of pints of that stuff and began acting like a raving lunatic. They had to ship him off to Essondale for quite a while to get over it. It was too bad. He was really a good engineer otherwise."

THE STATIONS HAD a distinctive appearance, and a smell even more distinctive. Built near the water on pilings driven down for footings, their timbers soon became saturated with oil from the whales they rendered down. Coal, their prime fuel, was piled high on the wharves to accommodate both the ships and the boiler house, which supplied steam power to run the station, and electricity to light it. The product of their endeavour was whale oil, and it was stored in large vertical tanks behind the stations, connected by pumps and pipes to the pierhead for delivery to the ships that transported it south to market. Gun powders and primers required by the whaling ships were stored in a powder shed, remote from work areas.

The station buildings were timbered and covered with corrugated iron; the sheds and houses were framed and clapboard-covered. Water was usually piped in from a convenient high-level stream or dam, and stored in large, wooden, water tanks which provided gravity feed to the houses and hose points. High-pressure service and fire points were supplied through steam-driven pumps. Outhouses were built on the outer end of piers that lay offshore, and steam heat was laid on to some of the buildings, while coal-burning stoves and heaters sufficed for the rest. Little consideration was given to creature comfort, as the station operated only during the fair weather months from April to late October, but the company made sure that accommodations for the station crew and management were favourably situated for a fair wind and a garden patch to grow fresh vegetables.

Such concern for good, fresh food did not extend to the food the whalers ate. All meat and vegetables had to be shipped up from Victoria on the station tender. Vegetables often arrived dried and wizened, and Charlie Watson recalled, "Bad meat had to be the bane we all suffered without recourse. Oh, I remember once, a bunch of the boys showed the company just what they thought about it. My God, it was funny! Bill Rolls was manager at the time, and we and the *Grant* were tied up at the dock, taking on coal and supplies, when the *Gray* arrived with meat and supplies for the station. Well, you know how they carried the meat in those days—hung on hooks out on the open deck. Both the *Gray* and the *Prince John* had their boilers and engines aft, and, of course, that was where they hung the meat. The heat and soot ripened it till it was oozing slime and black with blowflies, hardly appetizing, even for people like us who had been waiting weeks for its delivery. The cooks from both ships had been given permission to take their meat at the pierhead, and got several of the deck crew to give them a hand. But once they saw the state it was in, they told the boys to heave it over the side into the chuck.

"This was the final insult to our crews. They had carried that rotten stinking mess from the slings over to the ship, the ooze dripping down over their clothes and hands. Then they were told to dump it over the side. Realizing the company was going it cheap rather than put in a proper meat locker on the *Gray* or have it shipped by a company with refrigeration, they decided it was time to show their displeasure. Keeping the rotten

quarters of beef on their shoulders, they marched all the way up the dock to the station office and stalked inside, where they threw it right through the manager's plate glass door and left it lying on his carpet!"

Charlie roared with mirth as he recalled the incident, shaking his head slightly as he slapped a large paw down on his knee. "Oh, my god. There was a stink about that! If I recall rightly, they deducted the costs of repairing the door from the sailors' pay. But I'll say this for Rolls, he didn't fire anyone. After all, we all suffered when supplies were short.

"When we were desperate enough we'd even try whale meat! The Chinese usually cut some large pieces of meat off the Sei or small Finbacks, and left these hunks to hang till the outside turned black. More than once, when only salt beef or pork were our alternatives, we bartered with them for some of this. If you trimmed off the blackened meat and sliced the remainder into steaks or roasts, and cooked it over a slow fire, it was as good as some of that stringy beef, and tasted about the same. Of course, we always tried our hand at fishing or hunting when the opportunity presented itself, but if you're busy chasing whales there isn't much time left for anything else."

NADEN HARBOUR, BUILT in 1912, was typical of most stations built before World War II. Each station had its slipway, a stoutly timbered and planked ramp that led up out of the water to the work decks and the buildings housing the rendering equipment, grinders, and driers required to convert the total whale into useful saleable products. Steam winches, fitted with heavy wire cables, dragged the whale up the wetted ramp, or whaleslip, till it reached the high

Naden Harbour Station

water mark. The flensers climbed aboard the still-moving whale to begin slicing the blubber into strips with their long, wooden-handled, curved, flensing knives. These strips started at the head area and extended the full length to the tail, where the wire cable had been attached to haul the whale ashore. At the head end of the strip, a hole for the hook line was cut in. The strip of blubber was slightly undercut at the head end to allow it to fold back over itself. When it was pulled by the hook line from the stripping winch, it peeled back for the whole length of the whale with a sharp cracking sound that was not unlike that of an under-ripe banana being peeled.

Each strip was hauled up to the cutting deck and hacked into small chunks, then fed into the rendering kettles. The carcass was pulled up to the meat floor, where it was butchered into reasonably small chunks and placed in pressure cookers to render off the oil. Steam-powered saws cut up the bone. If the catch was a Sperm whale, the spermaceti was baled out of the head box, and the digestive tract was examined for ambergris.

After the cookers and kettles had rendered off most of the available oils, the bones were separated from the meat and stored on a bone pile, ready for grinding into bone meal during a lay day, or at the end of the season. The meat was ground, then dried in either flame-type or steam-jacketed rotary kiln dryers. In some stations, this dried meal was ground again to bring it down to the consistency of a powder, and was mixed with either the whale blood, which had also been dried and ground to a powder, or with the bone meal, to supply the various needs of the whale product market.

Although all were similar, each station had its own unique characteristics. Win Garcin spent many school summer holidays at Rose when his father was station manager, and he remembers, "Rose Harbour was mostly built on muskeg. There were deep pilings sunk to support the station and the boardwalk. If you got off those boardwalks, you'd sink up to your knees in muskeg and water. You couldn't wander too far away at Rose!

"There were flowers everywhere. Forget-me-nots, bluebells, snowdrops, and many others whose names I don't know. There were wild berries, huckleberries, blueberries, and wild strawberries. Underfoot was moss, lush moss, ankle deep and alive with shrews, moles, and all kinds of insects. The bushes and flowers were alive with bees, and the trees alive with birds. The place sang with nature's music. So warm and secure. The huge trees stood solid and tall against the sky, and the eagles. . . Hundreds and hundreds of them, wheeling and diving, swooping and gliding silently away up in the sky. I used to get the watchman's boat and row around, looking at all the various small islands and rocks. There were seals, sea lions, gooney birds, and sea parrots. You know the ones, with big webbed feet, short fat bodies, black feathers, and an orange beak like a parrot. Then there were lots of muskrats, mink, otters, and fish, lots of fish and deer everywhere. I believe there were also cougar and wolves up in the mountains, but I'm not sure, and lots of black bears. Then we had cats, lots of wild cats. You know, domestic cats that had gone wild. I guess people left them behind at the end of the season, and the cats just wandered off into the bush and managed to survive on all the rodents that are there.

"We caught a cat while I was there. It had wandered into the station to gorge itself on whale meat and got caught in a rat trap, so I was given the job to deliver it to Cat Island. I don't know the island's real name, but locally it was known as Cat Island, and was a small bit of land a couple miles away from the station and well enough off shore so the cats couldn't get back again. I rowed out there with the cat secured in a net bag, hissing and growling at my feet, where I could keep a good eye on it. It was really wild and quite big, but once I got it ashore and cut the lashings on the net, it didn't stay to argue but bolted for the trees. There seemed to be enough food for them all on that island; I could hear them hissing and growling in the bush, but could not see a solitary one."

The Dance of the Whales

WILLIAM HAGELUND

◆ ◆ ◆ ◆ ◆ ◆ ◆

Author, age 17, aboard whaler Brown, *1941*

IN 1941 I WAS a crewman on the *Brown*, hunting whales out of Rose and Naden Harbours for one season. It was an exciting time, and memories of those six months on a whaler still remain with me. There was one favourite story of that experience that my young sons often asked me to tell as they settled in to go to sleep. With a certain literary license on my part, our boys knew it as "The Dance of the Whales." Few people have seen this phenomenon, and never have I come across accounts of it written, but it was perhaps the most thrilling sight I have ever witnessed. If I were a painter, I could paint its details in vivid shades of colour, for the picture of it is still etched in my mind.

It was during the latter part of the afternoon watch, on a day that had been wet and squally, and I was cold and miserable as I stood my trick on the wheel. Finn John, the mate, was smoking his old stubby pipe, scanning the ocean as we rolled along on an outward sweep to skirt a northerly storm front that had kept us in its frigid grip all day. My eyes automatically came up from checking the compass to search the horizon opposite the direction the mate had swung his head. I snapped alert as my weary eyes spotted a strangeness there that warranted greater concentration.

To the southwest, the storm clouds were lifting and breaking apart as the wind backed around to that quarter. Fingers of sunlight poked down through these rents in the clouds to illuminate the grey heaving sea, turning the cresting waves a translucent green, and their foaming tops a milky white. Between these shafts of warm yellow were the dark curtains of rain squalls sloping down to the sea. What had caught my eye were small dark shapes that appeared and disappeared in those dark areas of the rain squalls. Undoubtedly fish-shaped, they were so far away that only once in a while could I actually see their tails. This placed them well over five miles away, and the only fish I knew that could be seen five miles off were whales. But I'd never seen whales behaving like this before. Almost a hundred feet in length and as many tons, they were propelling themselves up, completely out of the water.

I can not recall what sort of hail I made to get Finn John's attention, but when he turned to look, they were gone. He looked back at me, a little bemused, after scanning the area for a good five minutes through his binoculars without sighting a thing; even the sunbeams had disappeared. But he showed respect for my judgment and keen eyesight by hauling the ship around to a heading I indicated and, still at cruising speed, we moved towards that distant spot where the two winds came together.

Twenty minutes later we were amongst the rain squalls, and the wind tore the clouds apart with a fury that rent the silence with several long rolls of thunder. It was like the beat of drums, signalling that the curtains were rolling back and the play beginning. Sunbeams poked down onto the sea ahead of us with a brilliance that caused my eyes to water, the dark vertical lines of the rain squalls retreated northward, and the heaving, cresting sea came alive with colour. Then, before us, not more than ten or fifteen cables off, the surface of the sea erupted as sleek black whales nearly as big as our ship hurled themselves up out of the water, some standing as high as our mast, their tails beating the surface into a frothy foam to maintain their momentary posture.

Never had I seen anything like it. Finn John got so excited he literally jumped up and down. Pulling his pipe out of his mouth, and tearing off his hat, he beat it against the weather dodger of the bridge as he roared at me, "Jesus Christ, God almighty! Vill you look at those god damn sulphur bottoms yump and dance!"

He rang down for slow speed, but there was no need to call anyone up; the noise made by the whales had brought them all out from the supper table. There must have been a dozen or more whales in sight at any one moment, and as they dropped back into the sea, others took their places. God only knows how many whales were there...perhaps a hundred. Some of the smaller ones leaped so far out of the water I could see the horizon under their tails, and they terminated their leap in a curve that brought them back to the surface in a thunderous fountain of spray as they landed full length. Sometimes they would rise together in pairs, facing one another, and pause like two huge dancers before our startled eyes, their tails beating the sea into a froth that rumbled louder than any propeller rising to the surface.

Bounding up to the bridge, Louis Larsen, our skipper, scowled over at the whales like a tiger held at bay, his jowls quivering, his mouth opening and closing, and his hands clenching and unclenching on the handle of the telegraph. His gunner's instinct to let fly with a couple of harpoons warred with his master mariner's regard for our old ship's aging gear.

Caution won out and, ordering John to skirt the pod of Blue whales, he began looking for more suitable whales for our taking. The display lasted less than fifteen minutes, then the sea became strangely silent. Before anyone could retire, however, we sighted several Humpbacks breaching to starboard, and pounced on them so swiftly they were lashed alongside before we went to our supper. On our way into the station, we heard that the crew of the *Black* had not resisted the temptation when the pod of Blues had surfaced near her, and they were now returning to repair her windlass and replace the whole length of her mainline. There was no doubt they rued their impulsiveness.

During supper, Finn John attempted to explain the phenomenon we had seen by stating the whales were merely throwing themselves out of the water to create an impact of sufficient force to dislodge the encrustations and parasites they hosted on their skin. He said these parasites became more active and worrisome to the whales the further inshore, to the warmer and less salty waters, they came.

But Jacques-Yves Cousteau, in *The Whale, Mighty Monarch of the Sea*, states that both Finback and Blue whales couple by facing together like humans, and, to achieve this, they swim up from the depths together, trying to achieve penetration and climax before reaching the surface. I believe that what we had seen was the grand finale, after climax had been achieved, and the inertia of their swift passage upward rocketed them above the surface, where the tail wagging was a burst of ecstasy, signalling fulfillment of this great desire.

Perhaps someday the dance of the whales will be performed within range of a camera, and this amazing spectacle will be recorded for all to behold. Nothing less would convey the true magnificence of these great creatures.

THEY DON'T MAKE 'EM ANYMORE DEPT: FRANK OSBORNE

Jim Spilsbury

I SUPPOSE MOST OF us can look back through our earliest memories and recall one, two, or three "unforgettable characters" whose influence has been felt throughout our lives. Right now I am thinking of Frank Osborne, and I cannot put aside any story of my early years up the Coast, particularly around boats, without bringing him into it. My earliest recollections of Frank were based mainly on his manner and appearance. He was reasonably tall but stooped, moved slowly and deliberately, and seldom spoke except to answer in a monosyllable or a grunt. He was stooped, I guess, out of habit, as he was always bending over a lathe or a drill press or a forge in his machine shop in Lund. He never moved quickly or without deliberate decision because he spent most of his waking hours in close proximity to operating machinery and moving belts and spinning flywheels. The fact that he retained all his limbs, fingers, and toes, had both eyes, and bore no visible scars, attested to his "think first" attitude.

There was a certain omnipotence to Frank's presence which was enhanced by his personal appearance. He always wore dark clothes. They may originally have been dark blue overall material, but were always so saturated with oil, grease, and coal-dust that the effect was black. He wore a very old, battered, black, greasy felt hat. He was bald, but this didn't show as he always wore the hat. His face was generally as black and greasy as his clothes. If he ever did remove his hat, which he had the good manners to do in the presence of a lady, I was always surprised to see how white his head was. His shop was very poorly lit, and you could be standing quite close to Frank and not notice him. Only the whites of his eyes would show up until you got accustomed to the gloom. He did have electric lights, but they were very small and concentrated just over the working

area of each machine. In the blacksmith shop part he said he wanted it dark so he could see the colour of the metal he was tempering in the forge. I got to love the smell of blacksmith's coal smoke mingled with the smell of the dog-fish oil he used on all the cutting tools.

His manner sometimes appeared rude to those who didn't know him. To those who knew him well, he was an extremely kindly man, just not easily excitable or ready with an immediate response. Once again, this was partly due to his vocation. He would be sitting crouched over a lathe with belts flapping, smoke spiralling off the lathe tool, and long silvery metal turnings dropping to the floor, and some anxious individual would enter the shop and go and stand expectantly beside him and try to get his attention, probably something about his boat engine that was needing repair, but Frank would not take his eyes off his work for perhaps five or ten minutes, or until the cut was finished, when he would reach up and release the chuck, take the work out of the lathe and throw it on the floor, spit a long, accurately directed stream of tobacco juice down through a 10" by 10" square hole in the floor about ten feet away, turn slowly around to the individual, look over the top of his glasses at him, and grunt, "What do YOU want?"

Whatever the man's problem, providing it was a mechanical one, Frank would invariably take care of it, but only in his own good time and after the customer had come to the full realization that he'd be looked after when his turn came. If the man was patient and kept quiet, Frank would stop what he was doing and look after the man's requirements on a first priority basis. If he liked you, nothing was too much trouble. I learned this lesson very early on and went out of my way to be respectful and polite, and over the years I got the feeling that Frank treated me more like a son, probably because he had no children of his own. I respected the relationship. As a kid I loved nothing better than an excuse to spend time in the machine shop watching Frank work and, whenever there was an occasion, talking to him.

Once Frank told me about his early life and I wish now that I had paid more attention. Apparently he was an orphan, brought up in a monastery somewhere in the Ozarks or in that general hillbilly area of the United States. He worked on a farm and learned his blacksmith trade as a kid while at the monastery. Anyway, he wound up on the coast of British Columbia and settled down at Lund before the turn of the century, where he started a blacksmith shop and then a machine shop, both of which were badly needed in those days. He was a real creative genius, and very advanced for his time. He designed and built his own marine engine, the F.P. Osborne Heavy Duty Marine. He produced and sold two basic models—the Osborne 7 Horse Power Single Cylinder and the Osborne 14 Horse Power Two Cylinder. I seem to remember they bore a resemblance to the Atlas Imperial built in the United States at that time. In order to produce these he even operated his own foundry, right in the shop. I would guess that he probably ceased manufacturing them about 1925 or so, when heavy duty small marine engines went out of style. I can remember seeing them in quite a few of the local fishing boats. After that he invented, or at least designed, the first gasoline-powered boomstick borer, and these became widely used all over the coast for many years.

ONE TIME I came into Lund after I had been absent for a few weeks, and the whole appearance of the shop had changed. There was a big, new, painted sign over the door proclaiming F.P. Osborne to be the "Authorized Agent for DEUTZ Diesel Engines." More signs were posted around the shop. In front of the office, just out of its crate, was a shining new sample of the Deutz Marine engine. Some salesman had done a real job on Frank, and all he could talk about was this marvelous new "High Speed, Two Cycle Diesel" that he was offering.

But that was not all. There had been a much more drastic change which I found very upsetting. He had done away with his old faithful 5 hp vertical Fairbanks-Morse distillate stationary engine with the make-and-break ignition that had run so faithfully for so many years, turning all the wheels and pulleys and the slapping leather belts in the whole machine shop. In its place was a new, green, German diesel which was making a loud and piercing screaming noise as it supplied power for the shop. I asked Frank about it. He took me outside so we could get away from the noise, and launched into an enthusiastic lecture on the wonders of these new machines. This particular one was quite innovative. It had two horizontally opposed cylinders on a single crank, and turned up at quite high revs. Frank said it would run all day on a beer-bottle full of diesel fuel, there was nothing to wear out, and it would run for ever—everyone should have one. All this effusiveness was quite out of character for him, and I can only surmise what kind of salesman had administered the treatment. The old shop didn't seem quite the same after that.

It was a few months later before I came back to Lund, and to my surprise the old Fairbanks-Morse was back in place and going "Chuff Chuff Ha Ha Ha Chuff Ha Ha" just like it used to. There was a large hole in the back wall of the shop near where the Deutz had been sitting. Frank wasn't saying much, but after pressing him for an explanation, he told me the story. The Deutz ran just like the man said for several weeks. Then one lunch hour Frank had gone up to his house, directly behind the shop, when he heard the engine making an unholy noise and getting louder and louder. He was on his way down the hill about as fast as he ever moved, when the Deutz met him.

It had jumped right off its base and gone through the cedar board wall, and "liked to chase me back up the hill," as Frank put it. There was a very plausible technical explanation for its behaviour. Being a so-called two-cycle, it got its combustion air from the base of the engine on compression. For some reason, a quantity of lubricating oil and unburned diesel fuel had accumulated in the base over a period of time. This accumulation got sucked in along with the air and ignited in the cylinder, and it ran faster and faster since the governor no longer had control of the fuel supply. As the speed picked up, so did the amount of surplus fuel increase till the flywheels burst and the engine practically disintegrated, but not until it had succeeded in winding up all the old leather belts and pulleys in the shop, leaving the place in a complete shambles. Needless to say, all the signs had come down too, and the sample engine was gone from the floor. The subject was not discussed again. Frank was not given to that kind of mistake.

On one of my next trips up the coast I called in at the B.C. Forestry Station at Thurston Bay. The Forestry Department operated a large shipyard and machine shop here, and did almost all the maintenance and repair work on the fleet of Forestry launches. Bill Swan was the foreman in charge in those days. I was wandering around in the shop, admiring all the racks of spare engine parts etc., when I saw a small object that got my curiosity going. It turned out to be a siren off a police Harley-Davidson motorcycle. It had a small grooved pulley on the end of the shaft, which would be engaged with the side of the front tire on the bike when in use. Bill noticed my interest and picked it up to demonstrate it by holding it on the leather belt on the hydro generator. It instantly wound up to a piercing scream, and I decided I needed it badly for my business. Having no real use for it, Bill gave it to me. I ended by mounting it on a bracket on the top of the wheelhouse of *Five B.R.*, driving it by V belt from an old Ford Model T starter motor. I used it for years to announce my arrival at a camp; it became the signal that the Radio Boat was in harbour.

It was for the purpose of getting some machine work done on the bracket that I took it in to Frank Osborne's shop. As usual he was working at the lathe, the old Fairbanks-Morse was going "Chuff Chuff Ha Ha Ha" etc., and as usual Frank didn't look up from his work. I had the police siren in my hand, and I had a bright idea how to get his attention. I just reached over and held the friction wheel against the drive belt of the old Fairbanks and it produced a most ungodly yowl that could be heard all over Lund. The effect on Frank was spectacular. He jumped off his stool and headed straight for the Fairbanks. I was standing right in his path and actually held the siren up in front of his face so he could see what it was. It was still yowling. He knocked me over in the process of getting to his old engine, which he proceeded to shut down by closing valves and pulling wires off, and then throwing the drive belt off. Finally everything in the shop wound down to a dead stop, but the siren in my hand was still giving off a low moan. Then he turned around and took a harder look at me and said something like "Mother of Christ, what the F—k was that?" I guess he was still edgy after the Deutz incident.

To ALL OUTWARD appearances Frank was deadpan serious about everything, without so much as a flicker of a smile, so most people would not attempt to joke with him. In his own way he really enjoyed a good joke but just didn't show it. Otherwise he would never have put up with some of the things I did. The following story is a good example.

This happened only a few months after I bought the *Five B.R.*, when I encountered my first serious mechanical failure with the new vessel. For tractive power Bob Weld had converted and installed a 20 hp "Cletrack" tractor engine coupled to an old marine clutch and reverse gear which was too small for the job. One time when I went to go astern the drive shaft broke and left me dead in the water. I found it was quite a jagged break, and providing I went ahead, the propeller thrust would force the broken ends together and I could proceed very slowly without it slipping. So I pointed her in the right direction and, with my fingers crossed, kept her coming ever so gently all the way down the coast. I daren't stop, but kept going till I reached Lund where I executed a dead stick landing and with the aid of pike poles and shouting, got her alongside Frank Osborne's

machine-shop float at Lund. I expected to have to buy a new "Paragon Reverse Gear," which would cost about $350, but Frank said, "To Hell with them. They ain't any better than the one you just broke." He said he'd build me a better one. It would only take two or three days, and he guaranteed it would not cost over $100. So that is what we did.

At the back of the shop lay the remains of Frank's old red Nash touring car which was wrecked when he drove off the gravel road in a fog (partly alcoholic) on his way back from the Powell River beer parlour. He took the rear end and differential gears out of it and used these as the heart of a reversing gear by putting a drum and brake mechanism on it. The principle was much like that behind the friction bands and planetary gears in the old Model "T" Fords. It provided me with 100 percent reverse action. To all this he added a simple clutch which he built up of odd parts. He worked without plan or measurements, but everything turned out perfect and it lasted me the life of the boat. It was now the third day and the job was all but finished Saturday night.

Sunday morning we went to work as usual, but when I got to the shop, Frank was doing something else. He said, "Hell, this is Sunday. We ain't gonna work every day. It ain't good for a guy. Today we're gonna play a bit. I'm gonna make you a cannon for your boat. Every boat should have a little cannon." He was quite serious. He already had a short length of bronze propeller shaft in the lathe and was in the process of turning it down into a beautiful replica of an old-time brass cannon. He bored it out with a ½" drill and then drilled the nipple and attached the gunnions. He found a solid teak board from which he fashioned a gun carriage, adding two axles and four brass wheels. He polished it in the lathe using jeweller's rouge, and the whole thing was a joy to behold. It was finished by noon. He said that this was for real, and all we needed was some gun powder and he would show me how to use it. He sent me over to see Gerald Thulin at the Lund Hotel. His father, Fred Thulin, had owned an old Winchester 44-40, and Frank thought there were still some of the old black powder cartridges around. He was right, and Gerald gave me a handful of them, which we then proceeded to unload. Frank was extremely cautious in handling the powder, and felt he had to instruct me in every detail, even though I tried to tell him that, as a kid, I had made little guns and used lots of black powder which Dad had for loading his own shells. But Frank ignored my protests entirely and insisted on lecturing me in painful detail on the handling of explosives. He even made a cute little brass measuring cup with a teak handle so I could put the precise amount of powder in the barrel each time. He said, "Now one measure is enough, but if you want an extra large bang, then you could go to one and a half, but no more than that, do you understand?"

Well, that afternoon we took the little cannon down on the float and fired it time after time until Frank was satisfied that I knew how to handle it. The noise attracted quite a crowd for a Sunday afternoon and Frank suddenly realized he didn't want to be seen by his customers so frivolously engaged, so he left me to it. Also, we had run out of powder. I told him I would go over to Savary and get a 1 lb. canister that Dad had stored away, and that when I came back that evening I might fire it off a few more times if he didn't mind. He said no, it was OK, but remember—"Not more than one and a half measures, and be damned careful where you point it if you are using any slugs." I said "Yes, yes Frank, don't you worry. I'll be careful." And then, as an afterthought, he said, "Be sure you tie a rope on it in case it jumps overboard on you. It has quite a kick." I promised this would be done. His intentions were of the best, but I was getting a little tired of being treated like an inexperienced kid.

While I was over at Savary, I had an idea that rapidly developed into a plan of action to get Frank's goat. Stored away at the back of the property, Dad had a part box of 20 percent dynamite that we had been using for road building. I picked up two sticks, a detonator cap, and a length of fuse, and went back to Lund for an evening's entertainment.

I would make Frank think the cannon had blown up! I would plant the dynamite on the rocks in front of the shop, set it off, and when Frank came down I would hide the barrel of the cannon and show him just the carriage on the rope and see what he would say. I never expected it to get any further than this, but things worked too well and I found I had started something I couldn't control. Here was the set-up.

This part of Lund was on a very small bay, with a few houses, the machine shop, Dan Parker's one-man sawmill, Hugo Johnson's little marine ways, and then the old Malaspina Hotel and Government wharf, arranged in that order, in a rough semi-circle. Frank lived in a little house directly above and back of the machine shop, with a steep set of stairs leading up to it. Out in front of the shop, exposed at low tide, was a large pile of rocks that had been left there after the beach was cleared for the marine ways. The shop itself sat on pilings.

The tide was out far enough to dry the beach and was still dropping. I placed the dynamite by a rock that was out almost at the geometric centre of the semi-circle of the bay, so the sound of the shot would be well-distributed. I covered the dynamite with a bucketful of moulding sand from the old foundry, figuring this would be safe and produce no shrapnel. Then I attached a three-minute fuse. Before lighting it, however, I went over to Hugo Johnson who was taking advantage of low tide and was caulking some seams in the bottom of a boat. I told him roughly what I had in mind, and asked him if he could move over to the other side of the boat until the charge went off. He seemed to be pleased at the prospect of pulling a joke on Frank, and willingly complied. Then I had one further idea. I knew that Frank, at this time of night, would be listening intently to his favourite radio program, and he would probably be wearing headphones, so he might not hear the dynamite. I thought I better do something that would ensure getting his attention. His radio was a special one that I had built from scratch to be run entirely off the 32-volt bank of batteries that Frank had in the machine shop, and a special pair of wires came all the way down the hill to connect to the batteries. I decided I would slip into the battery room and disconnect the wires the instant the shot sounded. As things turned out, this could be described as overkill.

It was a Sunday evening and nothing was moving. The weather was dead calm, not a breath of wind to make a ripple or rustle a leaf. I double checked. Everything was set. I lit the fuse, ran in and took up my position in the battery house, and, with the wire in my hand, I waited. And I waited. It was the longest three minutes I could remember. I was beginning to think I had a misfire on my hands. And then—BLAM! and the whole building shook. Loose pieces of glass fell out of the old shop windows, and I involuntarily yanked the wire off as my feet left the ground. The noise it made was appalling, and for the better part of a minute echoes were coming back from the hills around. I fumbled round in the dark and reconnected the wires, then made my way down to the boat as quickly as possible.

Things started to happen. Porch lights came on, dogs were barking all over Lund, and gradually more and more people appeared, carrying bugs and flashlights, and generally heading down to the dock area. I looked up to the house and could see Frank out there busily pumping up and lighting a Coleman gas lantern. When he got it going to his satisfaction he reached up and jammed his old black hat on his head and started down the steps with the Coleman sizzling. I didn't have long to wait now, and I'd better have my story ready! My nerves were on the edge of panic. I think the only thing that saved me at this time was hearing the methodical "Plink Plink Plink" as Hugo's caulking mallet resumed its cadence. At least there was one person around with his wits collected.

When Frank arrived I was standing on the float holding the piece of rope with the gun carriage attached, trying to look innocently bewildered by it all. Frank stuck the lantern in my face and examined me closely. My eyes were red and watering from trying to stop laughing, and he took this to indicate a state of partial concussion.

"Are ya hurt kid?" was his first remark. I assured him I was OK but just a bit "Shook up."

"What happened to the cannon?" he said. I showed him the carriage.

"Wurrs the burrel?" I gave a helpless shrug and indicated I had no idea.

"Which way was she pointing?" he said.

"Out that way where you told me."

He considered that for a moment, then turned, and with his hand on edge indicated the exact reciprocal direction, across the clam beds and up to the sidehill. "She's gotta be thataways, and I'm gonna find her." With that he started to wade across the mud, searching with the gas lantern. He went right to the beach but didn't find it.

By this time quite a number of people had turned up. Some just inquisitive, some concerned and helpful, one or two quite hostile. They had not appreciated the cannonading exercise of the afternoon. Frank got them all organized in the search, and pretty soon the tide flats and the surrounding hillside looked like it was crawling with fireflies, with all the flashlights and lanterns. I stayed on the float to help direct people to the search area, all the while wondering how far this thing was going to go. Then Brooke Hogdson turned up. Brooke was the Dominion Government Telegraph Operator and Linesman. He lived about 4½ miles down the road from Lund, had heard the explosion, and came all the way up to Lund in his pick-up truck to find out what was going on. I knew Brooke well, having worked with him on the line, so I grabbed him by the arm and took him onto the boat and into my confidence. I showed him the barrel I was hiding, and asked for his help. He said, "Leave it to me; I'll think of something," and departed with the barrel.

Among the many that showed up at the scene was Aleck Johnston, the Provincial Police constable stationed on the police launch *P.G.D.2*, at that moment moored about a mile across the harbour in Finn Bay. The explosion shook him out of his bunk and he rowed across the bay to find out what was happening. I thought I better take him into my confidence too, and he was good enough to keep the peace. I don't know how much longer the search went on under Frank's urging, but the tide was still dropping, and *Five B.R.* was in danger of going aground, so I took advantage of this to make my exit and tie up over at Finn Bay, but only after promising Frank I would be back in the morning to resume operations. He said he intended to get all the school kids out after class the next day. I could see this leading us further and further into trouble, but next morning it was all nicely taken care of, thanks to Brooke Hogdson.

Brooke still had the barrel in his pocket Monday morning when he met Dr. Lyons, who had just come up from Powell River to carry out a routine medical inspection of the Lund School. Brooke saw his opportunity, filled Dr. Lyons in on the details of the story, and asked him to plant the barrel in the school yard on his way in. When the kids came out for morning recess it was no time at all before one of them discovered the barrel. Everybody had heard about the episode by then, so he took it immediately to the teacher who appreciated the seriousness of the situation and detailed two of the boys off to take the barrel straight down to Frank Osborne. Frank simply couldn't believe it and went back to the school with the boys so they could show him exactly where they found it buried, muzzle down, breech up, in a patch of dry sand.

I met him when he came down to the boat, holding the cannon barrel gently in both hands and staring at it, shaking his head in disbelief.

"That school yard has to be a half a mile from here, and them trees it went over must be at least two hunnert feet high! For Chrisake how much powder didja put inut? Didja put more'n I toldja? Didja use the measure I made you?"

I admitted that I may have got carried away and put in more than he said, but he still couldn't accept that this would have wrought all the havoc it did.

"Wadja put inut fer a slug?" he demanded next. Well, I had made up a long and, I hoped, plausible story. I told him I couldn't readily find a suitable slug that would fit the barrel the way I thought it should, so I had decided to go first class and mould one out of babbitt-metal. I reminded him that he had been using the forge the day before and had left some babbitt in the ladle after pouring some bearings. He wanted to know what I had used for a mould. I admitted that this had been a bit difficult until I got the bright idea of using the gun barrel itself as a mould, first putting a wad of wax paper and moulding clay on top of the powder charge. That did it. He threw his hat on the deck and stamped on it and shouted, "For Chrisake you cant solder them things up and expect them to stand it! It's a wunner ya didn't kill yourself! and if she hadn'tabeen well made you wouldadone!" He said, "Looka this," and he took a pair of calipers out of his breast pocket and carefully gaged the barrel at several places in the bore and then said, with real pride in his voice, "She might be sprung a little at the breach, but the rest of her's as good as the day I made her!"

Then he allowed himself to reminisce a bit, shaking his head in wonderment the whole while. "My Gawd what an explosion! Why it shook the whole earth! Two of them dishes of the old lady's fell offen the plate rail and broke, and you couldn't see across the room for dust! — and you know what? It stopped the Goddam radio right while I was listening to it. It was a coupla minutes before I could get her going again, but I finally fixed her. I took my jackknife to those condenser plates and jist when I touched one of em she started up again. Here's your Goddam gun, I got work to do!"

By Monday afternoon things began to get awkward. Some knew the story and some didn't. Some were anything but pleased to have their sabbath disturbed. The schoolteacher, who was a serious type, delivered the class a long lecture on the dangers of explosives generally, and cannons in particular, and apparently used my name quite freely throughout. I left that afternoon for the north, and didn't return to Lund for at least a month. But to my amazement, the story of the cannon preceded me wherever I went. It was spread by the purser and crew of the Union Steamship boat, and all the towboat crews that called at Lund heard and spread the story. There were many versions. Some had it that I had loaded the cannon with two sticks of dynamite and blown the whole machine shop apart. As for Frank, he delighted in telling the story till the day of his death. I saw him many years later and the first thing the old man said was, "You remember that Goddamned cannon I made? Have you still got it?"

He never learned the truth, or if he did, he preferred to remember it his way. Bless him! Bless him!

Frank Osborne, my early friend and mentor

From *Spilsbury's Coast* by Howard White and Jim Spilsbury. Copyright © Harbour Publishing 1987.

the Day They Took Our Town Away

ALAN OMAN

"**W**HERE ARE THEY taking the houses?" I said.

"To Holberg," my mother said, her soft face like dough with a smile.

"*Why* are they taking them away?" I asked, putting my left foot into my right gum boot.

She shook her head, not really knowing.

"Will Spry Camp still be called Spry Camp when it's there?" I studied my boot, waiting for her response.

"It will be called Holberg," she said, her eyes on my boot too.

"Then where will Spry Camp be?"

"There won't be any Spry Camp."

I considered whether to change the gumboot to the right foot, or simply put the left boot on the remaining unshod foot. It made little difference anyway, as there were big holes in both toes, and the original shape of the black rubber had lost almost all its definition. "But Spry Camp is here now and if. . . ."

She cut me short. "It will just be part of Holberg," she explained. "They say it will be the largest floating town in the world."

That didn't make it any better for me. It upset me to think that the only place I had ever known would be absorbed, without question or any real observance, into some other place, somewhere down the inlet...that I would never see it again...who cares if it will be the biggest anything in the world!

"Why?" I said.

My mother shook her head. "Your gumboot is on the wrong foot." She went into the kitchen. I put my boots on the right way, then struggled into the final, most essential item of clothing, my stain-blackened life jacket.

ISTUMBLED INTO the warm kitchen, still bleary-eyed, squeezed my life-jacket-encased chest between the chair and table, poured canned milk on the waiting bowl of cornflakes, and cast a glance at my mother, who shoved another stick of wood into the yellow enamel stove.

"You're always so slow to get up in the morning," my mother said, looking at me. She always said things like that when the truth hurt most.

I ate my cornflakes. Through the kitchen window I could see the end of the raft on which our house rested, and, stretching point upon point into the blue distance, the tree-lined hills crouched atop themselves in the mirror which was Quatsino Sound.

"I don't want Spry Camp to leave," I said.

"What's special about here?" she asked. "It's just a logging camp. Everyone knew that the company would move it sooner or later." She hid behind a screen of flour smoke as she kneaded dough for the bread. "Anyway, there's not much you can do about it. It's already on its way."

SO I HURRIED through my cornflakes, in my own manner of hurrying, and went outside into the yard. Yes, there was a yard, a rectangle of left-over raft 15 by 30 feet, both playground and workplace. Across this yard I shuffled in my unawakened state, and along the side of the house on a single, bouncing plank, until I could see the long string of single-storey houses on rafts, like ours. The rafts were cluttered with extra sheds, an overflow of machinery and rope, disused baby buggies, and worn-out washing machines. Each house flew its flags of laundry, out to catch the occasional ray of sunshine.

In the distance, the tugboat that had come from Port Alice to tow away the company buildings and those that would follow the camp to Holberg, tugged and struggled to separate the floats from the shore, much like a dentist pulling teeth.

I went back inside, angry. "What about my memories?" I may not have said precisely that, but it was the essence of what I felt at the time, for until then Spry Camp had been the sum of my experience in the world. I didn't know yet there would be other memories of a childhood raft-life, of snaking up and down Quatsino Sound until each turn was as familiar as a neighbourhood street is to a city child.

So, "What about my memories?" I said, and my mother, punching down the unruly mound of bread dough, smiled and assured me, "No one can take those away."

"What about the man in the woods who sings? Will he be gone too?" I asked.

"He's going to Holberg." She covered the dough with a white cloth and put it on the shelf at the back of the stove.

"Is there a place for him to sing in Holberg? Like the rock where he sings here?"

TO GET THERE, we walked across the stiffleg that joined the rafts to the beach at the same time it held them away. We made our way gingerly across the green slippery log, fearing at any moment that sudden shift of the foot and, in we'd go, tumble splash, the first of at least three dunkings a day. If we made the crossing safely, I could run helter skelter down a winding pathway through a tunnel of tall trees, up and over their roots, and around the corner to a large granite rock with *nothing* on it, while all around the rank and relentless growth expanded sideways and upwards until everything was filled with a dripping green that was so solid as to be almost black. What joy in that open space, turning around and around in spinning circles, faster and faster until the treetops were a continuous line circumscribing a patch of blue sky until I fell down, a dizzy halt, and glad because I didn't have to worry about falling in the water.

From there the path continued, around a corner, to the sound of a guitar. "What is it?" I asked. "Music," my mother replied. But it was not music as I had known it until then. Music was a quavering, a rising and falling, a clearing and fading heard on the brown radio in a corner of the small living room. Music was the sound governed by the whims of distorted incoming signals as they dropped into our mountain-bounded world, bouncing from one peak to another, all the way from Los Angeles or Seattle, and seldom from Vancouver which was the station we were supposed to get.

This was a different music, when the man began to sing in a sure voice. "I want to see," I said. So we went along the path to where there were other people in the woods.

Or did we do that? Perhaps we went home, for I don't remember the man, though I am sure he wore a big white hat and high leather boots and a wide belt with a silver buckle. Or perhaps he was just another logger from the two-storey bunkhouses, carefully segregated from our end of the town, eyeing the married loggers' wives.

Why didn't people sing more often, I wondered? My father didn't sing, unless it was too early. "It's nice to get up in the morning, but it's nicer to stay in bed...." I would wince and look forward to the end of it, when I could go back to blissful sleep and my own dreams.

MY FATHER WOULD get up early in the morning. He liked it. We differed in that. He would be up before light to catch the crummy that took the men into the woods. A bull of a man, he was the hardest worker and the hardest fighter, always at odds with the bosses, the crummy, and anything else that was in the way. "One Punch" they called him sometimes, this man who knew the solutions of the fist if not of diplomacy—which is why he didn't often work for people. At least, not for long. It made things even harder in those days of the depression which had their own uncertainty; his temper made them less certain still.

In the morning the men would run for the crummy. They talked about it often, the arbitrariness of the rush and having to punch the time clock, hating to have to jump when they were told, but knowing if they didn't there'd be no job the next day, and perhaps never again.

"Why should I run for the goddam crummy," my father would curse. "Never work for any man if you can help it," he advised me.

No one liked the crummy, my father least of all. But he ran for it nevertheless, out to the woods to chop the tall trees in those brutal, still-early days of logging.

I remember the logs as they came whizzing down the skid and dropped into the salt chuck with a giant splash, the spray hanging in the air for an almost endless moment before falling back. I liked watching men in high caulk boots skipping from one log to another with long pike poles to push and cajole the logs into neat bundles or, later, to engage in the art of piling log upon log and stringing them with heavy cable to make an exquisite Davis raft that everyone admired for its ingenuity.

My father rowed me to the booming grounds on a silent Sunday, when the loggers fastidiously cleaned and groomed themselves in an affirmation of their humanity for one day out of the week, oiling boots, polishing, cutting hair, mending socks. We passed the bunkhouses on the way, me perched on the bow as the clinker-built boat fairly flew through the water at my father's strong strokes. Some of the loggers were still out on the promenade, strolling along the boards joining each of the rafts, saying hello with only the curtest of nods that gave no quarter, admitted no need.

We left the camp behind and slid through the water to where the skid road dangled over the booming ground, where tall pilings tilted at an angle above the reflective water. My father drove the boat faster and faster until we hit shore, digging into the molasses mud, and I jumped onto a huge pile of bark that was there, bark stripped from the logs by the speed of their descent into the water.

Firewood was always needed. It wasn't easy to get, even in a logging camp, in those days before chain saws. Here was slow-burning bark, to be had for the picking. My mother prized it for baking bread, so my father picked up the first man-sized piece and threw it into the row-boat...and then another, and another...until the boat was half full.

He paused, sweating a little, and pushed the rowboat off a bit so it wouldn't get impossibly stuck in the mud. Then he piled more and more onto the boat until, at last, the bark towered above the white hull like an overflowing ice cream cone.

I perched on top of the bark. My father heaved at the bow, pushing the boat out of the mud. He leaped and landed beside me as we floated outward...and sank downward, until I was in my father's arms and the boat was somewhere below his feet. The wet bark was too much for that little boat.

WOOD WAS A necessity for the kitchen, but for me it was a source of constant joy. The wood pile was my fort, my cave, my refuge from a scolding. And I loved the chopping block, the patterns made by the hundreds of blows of the axe. One day I sought to make those marks more permanent by outlining them in nails. So, diligently, I hammered, following each line with great care. When I ran out of patterns to copy, I made my own, until the top of the chopping block was a solid, shining plate of nail heads.

That was the first spanking I can remember. But somehow I was pleased enough with my handiwork that the spanking, and going to bed early without dinner, seemed not too insufferable a punishment. Anyway, I liked being on my own. There was always something to think about.

Like the day the killer whale came to the end of the inlet. It came bouncing and rollicking along, looking like a barrel pushing in and out of the water. I thought it was playing, but apparently it was lost and in danger of running aground on the mud flats. The men went out in their flimsy boats and shouted and waved their arms and sent it back down the inlet toward the ocean. I wished that it could stay for a while longer, that I could be allowed to swim out and play with it.

I ROWED BY THE time I was three, and learned to swim just as early, from accidental practice and apparent need. I learned quickly, mostly because of my father's teaching method, which consisted of putting a large plank in the water, throwing my sister and me into deep water some distance from the plank, and shouting at us to swim! The system worked. We survived the water, if not totally the terror.

For my mother it was a different story. I remember her learning, or, rather, *not* learning at the same time as us. For a woman raised in Quatsino with its watery way of life, she was curiously backwards about learning even the art of the dog paddle. My father tried to teach her, but where we children swam with a determined eye to our own self-preservation, my mother sank. She was hauled, kicking and complaining, back to the surface, only to be launched out again and again and again. Father's teaching method was never a success in her case.

I WATCHED THE LAST of the long string of houses as it receded into the distance. "What are we going to do?" I asked my mother as she checked the golden bread in the oven and decided that it was done. "Will we go to Holberg?"

"No," she said, and cut a slice off the first loaf of steaming bread, buttered it, jammed it.

I sensed a touch of uncertainty about her, perhaps the same feeling of rootlessness that I felt as we stared at the silent skid road, the empty booming ground, and the straggling, useless stifflegs along the shore where the town had once been. Nothing much to see now. I took the slice of bread and jam.

"Where will we go then?" I asked.

"Winter Harbour," my mother said. "At the ocean end of the inlet."

"Where the killer whale went?"

"Yes," she said.

"What will we do there?"

"Your father will go fishing and you will go to school."

It made sense to me that my father would become a fisherman. It was the only thing for a man who couldn't work for other men. I had heard him talk about the freedom of that life, and he had already bought a boat.

"When are we going?" I asked.

"In a little while," she said.

I took my bread and jam and went outside where my father had already attached an arm-thick rope to the raft. He started the boat's engine and paid out the line until it was tight behind the boat. The engine gained power and the raft began to move. The stiffleg fell away like a useless umbilicus. The shoreline became increasingly distant in barely perceptible stages.

I went to the back of the raft and watched the overhanging trees, the narrow line of rock visible above the tideline, the changing perspective of Spry Camp which now opened before me. I noticed the whorls behind the raft as it picked up speed, the raft sucking the water with it as it moved, until finally it abandoned even that aspect of the place.